Western Training

BEYOND THE BASICS

LAURIE TRUSKAUSKAS KNOTT

PHOTOGRAPHY BY
DAVE HAMRICK

Alpine
PUBLICATIONS
Loveland, Colorado

Western Training: Beyond the Basics
Copyright © 2006 by Laurie Truskauskas Knott

Library of Congress Cataloging-in-Publication Data

Knott, Laurie Truskauskas, 1957-
   Western Training : beyond the basics / Laurie Truskauskas Knott; photography by Dave Hamrick.
      p. cm.
   ISBN 1-57779-065-0
      1. Western riding. 2. Title.
SF309.3.K62 2005
798.2'3 pcc22

2004057079

The information contained in this book is complete and accurate to the best of our knowledge. All recommendations are made without guarantee on the part of the author or Alpine Publications, Inc. The author and publisher disclaim any liability with the use of this information.

For the sake of simplicity, the terms "he" or "she" are sometimes used to identify an animal or person. These are used in the generic sense only. No discrimination of any kind is intended toward either sex.

Many manufacturers secure trademark rights for their products. When Alpine Publications is aware of a trademark claim, we identify the product name by using initial capital letters.

This book is available at special quantity discounts for breeders and for club promotions, premiums, or educational use. Write for details.

Design: Laura Newport
Cover Photo: Chris Stuart and Dawn Stephens
Editing: Diane Borneman

1 2 3 4 5 6 7 8 9 0

Printed in the United States of America.

Contents

Dedicated to Joe Ferro—
without whom there would be no book.

To my twin sons, Don and Jon, and my grandchildren,
who have taught me as much as I have taught them.

And to John, who has made my life complete.

Foreword

Horses are more and more becoming companion animals rather than the working horses of days past. With that change, the art of training is no longer common knowledge. While in years past a trip to the local feed store would avail you of knowledge, tips or hints from several old cowboys just hanging around to pass the time of day, that is no longer the case. It is a loss indeed, and with that loss arises the need for a new source of knowledge. This book tries to fill that need and gives the backyard owner handy tips to make your horse a better working partner, knowledge that might otherwise only be gained by spending months with a trainer.

This book is aimed at the backyard owner who has a good grasp of basic horsemanship and whose horse is slightly past green broke, knowing the basics of walk, jog, lope, and halt. But a horse can do so much more. This book is easy to understand and will show you, step by step, how to progress slowly and easily to make your horse a better working partner. By understanding how a horse thinks, you will avoid many of the pitfalls faced by the average owner. When you get your horse's respect, he will be ready to listen to your requests. If he doesn't repect you, your horse will walk all over you and can become dangerous. You don't have to be a six-foot-tall cowboy to get and keep your horse's respect. Once you have that respect and then have control of your horse's body, you can teach him maneuvers beyond the basics. Only then will you have a horse that is truly a joy to ride and to work around.

My job as a farrier is made much more difficult when I work with a horse that doesn't stand still to be shod or trimmed. A horse that shoves people around is showing a lack of respect for his human handler. A horse that will not willingly pick up his feet and stand in one spot is showing his lack of respect. Manners on the ground go hand in hand with manners under saddle. When I ride, I expect my horse to respect my cues. That is the only way that I am able to enjoy my sport, which is team sorting and penning. A horse must know much of the knowledge that can be gained through this book, whether the owner is team penning, showing in pleasure or reining, or simply going down the trail. All of these horses must have knowledge that extends "beyond the basics."

Gary Hill
Professional Farrier

Acknowledgments

Once again, I must thank Joe Ferro of Grand View Ranch, Harwinton, Connecticut. He took the time to pass on his knowledge of how a horse thinks, and how to utilize that knowledge to train a horse correctly. He read every chapter of this book (before I submitted the finished manuscript) and gave me the confidence to put on paper what he taught me. Without him, there would be no book.

I would like to thank my sons, Don and Jon, for encouraging me to live a dream. For sending me to Texas to fulfill a lifelong dream of owning a beautiful horse facility where the weather is warm, the land is flat, and it doesn't snow. For twenty-five years, I put that dream on hold, choosing instead to raise my sons the best I knew. They rewarded me well—growing into wonderful, hard-working, polite, ambitious young men that I left behind in the snowy state of Connecticut. Not only did I leave them behind, but I left my No. 3 "Super Truck," a half-ton Chevy pickup (my other hobby), that my sons now race at Riverside Speedway in Agawam, Massachusetts.

Thanks also to:

Friends who read the final drafts of my chapters and gave advice and suggestions and encouragement.

My mother, Bernice Bunn, who has helped me with so many things over the years, and who moved to Texas to help once again and enjoy the good weather and friendly people.

Traci Phillips, who found me a photographer, and to Dave Hamrick for taking these photos on such short notice.

And again to Betty McKinney and the Alpine Staff who published this book, my first book, *Training the Two-Year-Old Colt,* and others.

Preface

My goal in writing this book is to give you, the reader, a better understanding of how a horse thinks and therefore, how a horse learns. Training a horse requires that you "think like a horse" and then "tell" or show the horse in a way that the horse can understand what is and is not acceptable behavior.

I worked with Joe Ferro of Grand View Ranch, Harwinton, Connecticut, for many years before venturing off on my own as a trainer and instructor. The day that I honestly understood how to train a horse was the day that Joe said to me, "Think like a horse. What did you just tell that horse?" (I forget exactly what I had done wrong, but it was something simple like letting the horse turn left when I'd asked him to turn right.) Joe said, "Think of what you just told that horse. You told him that he can go left rather than right. You told him that he doesn't have to respect you or obey your commands." As I opened my mouth to justify my actions (as so many people want to do), he said, "You will never make a trainer if you let a horse do that."

He walked away. The choice was mine whether to take what he said as helpful, constructive criticism, get mad at the horse for making me look dumb, or figure out how to make the horse obey my cues. I chose to take what he said as constructive criticism and sat on that horse's back until I understood exactly what Joe had said to me.

At that point, I became a trainer rather than a rider or a passenger. All of my "textbook" training went right out the door. I began to think of what I was telling a horse with every cue and every move that I made. No longer did I look for the neat, concise, textbook answers—such as exactly where I was supposed to put my hand or my leg to tell this horse what to do. I learned that you must put your hand, leg, seat, weight, and whatever else you might have wherever it would be the most effective. I used my aids in varying degrees until I found how or where an aid should be used to tell this particular horse how to perform exactly as I wanted him to at this point in time. I might have to adjust an aid, play with varying amounts of pressure or move the aid an inch—or a foot—higher or lower, more to the right or more to the left—until I got the response that I wanted. I might have to use an aid in a more exaggerated fashion, using more pressure, so that later I could lighten up on a cue and get the desired results. I learned that I might have to raise my rein hand eighteen inches above the saddle horn or that I might have to take my foot and tap the horse in the shoulder to get him to understand. Equitation applies more after a horse is trained. I learned that every horse is different—you use what works.

Once in a blue moon you get a nice, easy, textbook horse to train that obeys all the rules as they are written. It would be easy if every horse understood that leg pressure applied at point A meant to spin, leg pressure applied at point B meant to side pass, and leg pressure applied at point C meant to roll back. However, you are dealing with a living, breathing, very large animal that has a mind of his own. You cannot "program" a horse as you would a computer or make him go as you drive a car. You must talk to a horse in a language that a horse can understand.

It takes months of training to teach a horse to be "solid" and to respond to the light, almost invisible cues used on a finished horse. You must exaggerate a cue in the beginning, or use cues in a step-by-step program, until eventually you get the desired end result. Stop looking for textbook answers and adjust your cues until you find what works for you on that particular horse. Be fair and consistent. Reward your horse so that he understands that he has done as you desired. Much of my time is spent thinking, "How can I best tell this horse to respond to my cues, so that he obeys in a way that is acceptable?" If he makes a mistake, I think, "Did I do something wrong?" (*Not:* "This horse is so dumb. He'll never learn.") "Have I confused him? Did I use cues that were beyond his level of ability at this point in time? Should I back up a step? Is he only having a bad day? Why are we—this horse and I—not getting the correct results?" How can I make this better?"

Joe would often come out to the round pen and give me a one sentence answer to a perplexing problem; then he would walk away. He'd let me figure out the answer for myself. And so I learned, the hard way, to think, to learn, and finally to train. And you can too, if you will just stop and think about what you are telling the horse with every cue or move that you make.

Joe has probably forgotten more than most of us will ever know about horses. His son Roy won the first NRHA (National Reining Horse Association) reining class and rode many horses to AQHA Champions. Both father and son are still involved in raising top reining horses. Joe has known many great trainers of reining horses and also those of pleasure horses, halter horses, and even hunters. My first hunter that placed well was trained with his help. His favorite story is telling people about the time that a woman at a show asked me who had trained my horse. I said, jokingly, "A little 95-year-old man at the farm. He rides her every night and whacks her over the head with a two-by-four." While he never actually rode that mare (nor hit her with a two-by-four), he did tell me how to train her. From that mare, he taught me how to start colts the right way so that they would become well-trained members of the equine family. My first book, *Training the Two-Year-Old Colt,* is based on what I learned from Joe. He taught me how to start a colt by giving me colts to ride and simple guidelines to follow. If the colt messed up, it was because I wasn't clear in what I wanted. And so I learned to avoid that mistake in the future as well as how to fix the first colt's "problem." Joe taught me to train a reining horse using the same method, basically by putting my hours in the saddle and paying attention to what my horses "told" me. He always wanted to write a book, and so I hope, Joe, that this is the next best thing. I have put all that you have taught me and what I learned on my own in the pages of this book. In this way, the knowledge that you so willingly gave me can be passed on to all who read this book. Happy Training.

Laurie Truskauskas Knott
Trainer/Author, Silver Creek Farm

Introduction

As you read through this book, you'll notice I focus a little more on the reining horse, but what I've written applies to the pleasure horse, the trail class horse, the all-around show horse, or the all-around backyard or trail riding horse. Every horse will benefit from the more advanced training contained in these pages. If you have a young (or older) horse that only knows the basic walk, jog, and lope in a straight line, teaching him to move from leg pressure, to lift his shoulder, and to flex at the poll in response to rein pressure will give you the ability to move the various parts of his body. Should you go on to teach him some of the reining maneuvers, he'll need this base of training to learn those new and demanding maneuvers. If you show your horse, he'll need to learn to collect—or to drive his hind legs further underneath himself to lift and round his back—to travel in a frame with his face vertical to the ground as he slowly propels himself forward on a loose rein. Or if you simply want to have some fun with your horse and teach him to be a more willing partner with a bigger base of knowledge, you will also benefit by teaching your horse some of the exercises in this book.

Many of my clients have seen my horses and asked what I did to get them to be so truly broke. So I wrote this book, which follows my *Training the Two-Year-Old Colt* book, in hopes that others would benefit by what I've learned over the years. Remember that it takes months, not days, to train a horse so that he has a solid base of knowledge. Trying to cut corners is like trying to write a letter without using vowels. Start with the basics and add each new training segment in a logical, sequential manner. The more often you ride, the faster both you and your horse will progress.

Before you decide to head your horse towards a certain discipline, however, it is best to look at his conformation and trainability. And so, on to the first chapter.

CHAPTER ONE

Evaluating Conformation and Trainability

FORM TO FUNCTION

According to the *Merriam-Webster Dictionary,* conformation is described as the arrangement and congruity of parts (congruity meaning the correspondence between things). Choosing a horse with conformation that suits your chosen discipline will allow the horse to perform without undue stress to his body and legs. Correct conformation will help the horse perform with ease and keep him sound as he does so—thus form to function.

STUDY BLOODLINES

Look for a horse that has performance bloodlines. This will tell you if he has been bred to have the mind and the ability to perform. Look at his sire and dam, grand sire and grand dam, and even further back. If his parents or other close relatives have not performed in your chosen area, chances are that he will not be able to either. There is always the exception to the rule, but if you are looking to increase your odds of having a successful horse, start with the best that you can afford to buy or the best that you can afford to breed to. Study

past bloodlines. Study the horses that you like. Look at what bloodlines are doing well in the show ring today. Set yourself up for success.

As reining becomes ever more competitive, the horses capable of winning are becoming tougher. Years ago, if a horse showed a lot of speed, even if his form was not totally correct, he was able to place well. Today, a horse must not only show speed, he must show the correct form and also be pleasing to look at. A horse that jams his front legs into the ground when stopping will never score as high as a horse that drops his hind end close to the ground and paddles in a cadenced step in front, staying soft and light in the bridle. A horse that spins without keeping his hind pivot foot locked in place or one that hops or bounces around his spins will never outscore a horse that spins more slowly but does it with finesse and correct form. A horse that rushes through these maneuvers because he is scared or because he is too "hot" to accept the confines of training does not place as well as a horse that waits patiently for his rider's commands.

Watching a well-trained reining horse is a truly unique experience. These horses can drop their hind ends to get deep in the ground to stop and then perform high-speed turnarounds and rollbacks that will take your breath away. They can slide to a stop and then raise up out of the stop to back twenty feet in a perfectly straight line. What makes this truly impressive is that they do it on a loose rein, willingly, showing no signs of resentment. One wonders how they can stay sound year after year, slide after slide, spin after spin. This is where a good mind plus correct conformation, athletic ability, and the proper conditioning comes into play.

A horse that is higher in his rump than at his withers will not find it easy to curl his hind legs under his body to slide to a stop. This type of conformation predisposes a horse to stopping on his front end or jamming his front legs into the ground and bouncing to a stiff-legged halt. Straight shoulders and the matching straight pastern angles will give a horse a short, choppy stride; this is uncomfortable to sit to and gives the lope a choppy, hard-riding appearance. His front leg cannot extend past the angle (continued down toward the ground) of the shoulder. (See illustration on page 6.)

A horse with a thick neck and a thick throat latch will find it difficult to flex at the poll; doing so will hinder his breathing or even cut off his air supply entirely. His thick neck will also hinder his ability to balance himself. Light or weak muscling in the hindquarters will cause a horse to be more prone to injury than a stouter, correctly built horse. Weak muscling in the loin and hindquarters will decrease the length of a horse's slide, reduce the snappiness seen in a correctly performed rollback, and affect the speed of his turnarounds. These are all conformation problems that an animal can be born with and that training cannot change.

Conformation tells what a horse is naturally suited for. A horse's confor-

mation will give you insight into what a horse can perform the easiest, and therefore the most willingly. If he is naturally built to perform those maneuvers, he will be less likely to come up sore. A horse that comes up sore often will soon begin to resent those maneuvers that he knows will hurt him. Then, besides the physical or training problems that you might encounter, you must overcome the mental reluctance to perform those maneuvers as well. A horse will not want to perform, or try to perform, if it hurts him. With the amount of time involved in training a reining horse, it only makes sense to start with an animal that is naturally suited to hold up to the demands asked of him in such a career. In this way, the horse can stay physically sound and mentally happy.

Some horses can overcome a slight conformation "defect" and go on to prove themselves, but again, the majority will not. Increase your odds of success by choosing a horse with the correct conformation for the job at hand. Horses with conformation problems are constantly working against themselves. Their conformation hinders them as they try to perform and eventually they may refuse to perform at all. Training a horse that is conformationally suited to the job at hand—one with the bone, muscle and power in the proper places—will be easier on both you and the horse.

Once in a great while you may find a horse whose conformation goes against the rules—he should not be able to stop; he should not be able to change leads or any of the other maneuvers, yet he overcomes it all and goes on to be a top reining horse—but this is the exception rather than the rule. There will always be the unexplained exception to every rule, that one-in-a-million horse that proves the rule wrong.

READ HIS MIND

A horse's mind is a very important consideration also. A horse must not only be *able* to perform the maneuvers we ask of him; he must also *want* to perform them. While you can look at a horse and see his conformation, his mind or his willingness to learn is hidden behind a mask. Some horses do not retain what they have been taught from one day to the next. Others are unwilling to try even the most basic of maneuvers. You might train this type of horse to perform to a degree, but it is going to be a constant battle. This horse may quit on you at the most inopportune time—or refuse to perform at all.

Other horses are too "hot" to really accept the training process. They fly off the handle at the least little thing, bolting from unknown fears. They may resent the slow, controlled aspect of training and try to evade it at every chance. Hours and hours of training at home fly right out the trailer door when faced with the excitement of a horse show or of a new setting. Age and miles may help these horses somewhat, but by choosing this type of horse, you are setting yourself up for a long haul, working against the odds, and with no guarantees down the road. Although a certain amount of energy is required to perform the high speed turnarounds and snappy rollbacks seen in a well-trained reining horse, if that energy is not *easily* controlled, it will work against you much more than it will help you. It is always easier to push a quiet horse on than to bring a "hot" horse back. A well-trained reining horse shows little or no resistance. While any or all of these horses may have the conformation to perform, lacking a good mind to go with that good conformation will work against you just as much as, if not more than, bad conformation.

A horse with a good mind will work with you. He will try to decipher what it is that you want him to do. He will put his heart into trying to perform as you ask. He is attentive to your slightest shift in weight, the touch of a rein, the touch of a leg. He will gallop and then willingly come right back in hand, without blowing up or becoming resentful. With the right horse, one with a good mind and good conformation, you can go as far as your training ability allows. Your horse is built to do it right, and his mind makes him *want* to do it right. He may try so hard that he overdoes what his body is conditioned for. You will need to condition this horse properly so that he does not pull a tendon or muscle because of lack of fitness. But once properly fit and ready to work, the sky is the limit.

LOOK FOR ATHLETIC ABILITY

A reining horse, or any horse used for any of the other demanding sports, requires athletic ability. The horse must not be clumsy or lazy. He must be able to handle his feet and not get tangled up with his own legs when asked to perform. Watching a horse at liberty or in a round pen can often give you some insight into his natural ability. Asking a horse to roll back off the fence in a round pen will give you an idea of how he handles himself. If his legs get tangled up without a rider, how can you expect him to perform that same maneuver with a rider? Don't confuse a young horse that is at an awkward stage in his growth with a horse that is basically clumsy. Some colts may just need more time to grow up and mature, both mentally and physically. Others, however, will always be unable to perform all but the simplest of maneuvers.

Look for a horse that is balanced and light on his feet. A horse that has a massive front end and weak hindquarters will not stay sound when asked to "get into the ground" and slide or turn around or spin. These maneuvers require a strong loin, a strong stifle, and strong gaskin muscles. A horse holds himself in the ground with these muscles. Watch his bulging hind end muscles as he spins. A horse that is not strong in this area will become sore and then resentful. Once a horse begins to try to "save" himself from the pain associated with a given maneuver, overcoming it (mentally) will be difficult.

CONFORMATION

When choosing a prospective reining horse prospect, start at the head of a horse and work your way back, following these suggested guidelines.

Head

Look for a horse with a pretty head and an intelligent look to his eye. While you do not ride the head, you *do* need the intelligence that is located inside. The horse must retain what he is taught and not be resentful over these sometimes difficult and demanding maneuvers. The size of a horse's head should be in proportion to that of his body. The horse must use his head and neck as a balancing tool. A head that is not sized in relation to the rest of his body can hinder balance.

Eyes

Look for a horse with a soft, quiet eye. The eyes are the window to a horse's soul and can give you insight to his personality. The eyes should be large and set to the side of a horse's head. Eyes set this way allow a horse better vision. He will be able to see what is in front of him as well as to the side and behind him to a certain degree.

Look for a horse with a pretty head, clean neck, and intelligent look to her eye. (Misty Seven, owned by Laurie Truskauskas)

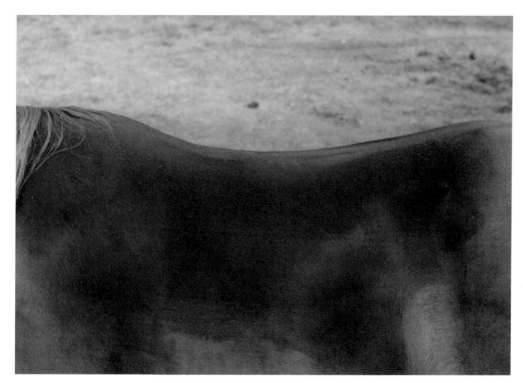

Be sure that your horse sweats evenly under the saddle. Uneven sweat shows that a saddle is pinching and cutting off the blood supply to the area. Many times, you'll see round, dollar-sized dry spots at the top of the shoulder blades by the withers. If so, the saddle is pinching and the horse will not be free to use his shoulders correctly. Try a different arrangement of pads or use a different saddle.

Nostrils

Large, elastic nostrils will allow the horse to take in, and then exhale, more air. A small nostril can cause a horse to choke as he tries to exhale; the air "bellows up" in the inner nostril since the small nostril cannot expand enough to let the horse exhale all of the built-up air. A reining horse is required to put in a maximum effort—loping, galloping, spinning, and sliding—for the duration of the pattern. A horse that runs out of wind will not be able to extend himself or give his best effort.

A horse with a pretty head is pleasing to look at. All other things being equal, a pretty horse will generally win over an ugly horse, human nature being the way it is. When faced with a pretty horse, wanting him to win is natural.

A horse needs large, elastic nostrils. (Trouble, owned by S. Bateman)

Neck

A horse needs a long, reasonably thin neck attached to his head to help to balance himself. This will not only help as he gallops or lopes, but will help him to balance when he spins or rolls back. A horse with a short neck lacks the agility and balance of a longer-necked horse. Most important, a horse needs a clean throat latch. He must flex at the poll and still be able to breathe easily. A thick throat latch can hinder or even cut off a horse's air when he is asked to flex at the poll. A horse with a "ewe" neck (sometimes called an "upside down" neck, since it looks as it was put on upside down) generally results in a high-headed horse that cannot or will not comfortably

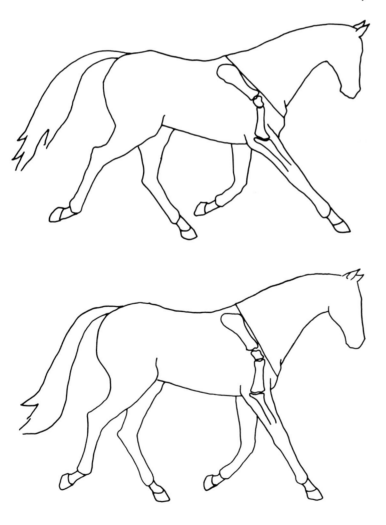

(Top) Good slope to the shoulder.
(Bottom) A straight shoulder shortens the stride.

flex at the poll and round his back. As discussed in the chapter on collection, a horse must flex at the poll to round his back and drive with his hindquarters. A horse that hollows his back and travels with his head in the air will have problems using his body to its full potential. He will have problems with almost all of the reining maneuvers.

Back

A horse needs to have a short back with a long underline. Look for a good slope to the shoulder and well-defined withers. A horse with "no" withers will not keep the saddle in place. Prominent, properly muscled withers give the ligaments and the muscles that attach the neck to the body of the horse more freedom to move. The horse can then exhibit greater flexibility and coordination and more freedom of the front end.

Overprominent withers, on the other hand, can make it difficult to find a saddle that will fit well without rubbing or pinching. A horse with a painful back will become sore and then resentful. Many training problems are blamed on the horse, when in reality a poorly fitting saddle is the culprit. Check to see that your horse sweats evenly under the saddle after a workout. Dry spots that show up are caused by the saddle pinching in that particular area, cutting off his circulation which doesn't allow that area to sweat. Saddle sores are caused by the saddle rubbing incorrectly on the horse and can take weeks to heal.

The Topline

A horse needs a short topline, only enough room for a saddle to fit comfortably. Lengthening the topline of the back (everything else staying the same) will push the withers closer to the horse's neck. This will change the angle of the shoulder from sloped to straight, providing the actual length of the back remains the same. A horse with a sloped shoulder can reach more not only when loping or galloping, but it will also help with his turnarounds.

A horse with a long back is more prone to back problems. The length of his back needs room to carry the saddle comfortably; anything else is wasted length. Consider this. Why do we frame the roof of a house with rafters and *then support the rafters with knee braces?* It is because a sixteen-foot span of rafters will not hold the weight of the roof without additional support. However, if the rafters were only two feet in length, additional support would not be necessary. The shorter length makes the rafters stronger. The same is true of a horse's back.

A short back, good shoulder, and long underline.

The Barrel

A horse's barrel should not be slab-sided or too light. He needs well-sprung ribs to give him plenty of room to hold the heart, lungs, and digestive system. The horse needs this room also for a large diaphragm so that he may increase his intake of air. Short, flat ribs decrease the vital capacity of a horse and therefore, his athletic potential.

Hindquarters

Strong hindquarters constitute a horse's motor, or where the power comes from. Although a horse's front legs do help to pull a horse forward slightly, most of a horse's power is gained by the strength of the hindquarters. Because of the joints involved in moving the horse forward (the hocks, the pastern, and the ankles), a weak "link" here will interfere with your

horse's soundness. Stifle and gaskin muscles that are not developed fully on both the inside and the outside of leg will also interfere with your horse's way of going. When fully developed both inside and out, these muscles help make your horse's leg travel forward in a straight line. A gaskin that is heavily developed on the inside of the leg, without the opposing balancing muscling on the outside of the leg will draw the leg in as he moves forward. The opposite—light muscling on the inside and heavy muscling on the outside—will cause the horse to travel wide. The stifle muscle is largely responsible for sending the horse forward and the gaskin muscle is mostly responsible for the course of the leg as it follows though the forward movement, provided, of course, that the bone structure is correctly aligned.

Power is generated in the horse's hindquarters.

Remember this image, if nothing else from this book!

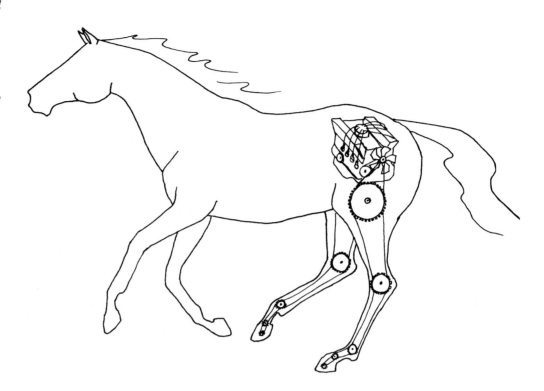

Hocks

A good hock is rugged looking and square in appearance, set neither too high nor too low. It should be clearly defined with no fatty appearance. A horse's maneuverability in his lope departures, spins, and rollbacks is greatly determined by the strength and quality of the hocks. The hocks give the tendons their springlike action. The tendons of the lower leg contract to set the horse in motion, and then pass through the pastern and the ankle before running through the back of the hock. This same energy or forward motion is then passed forward to the point of the stifle (located in the fore part of the hind leg, just below the flank). From here, the muscling is attached so that the energy created by the tendons goes from the stifle joint backward to the buttocks, and then forward over the topline of the hindquarters. This is why we say that a horse's power is located in his hindquarters.

Gaskin

A long gaskin muscle provides a maximum area for the attachment of the drive muscles (mentioned above) of the hindquarters. The muscles of a well-conformed horse should tie in well, being neither too slight nor too bulky. A horse that is too bulky often lacks the ability and agility to move quickly and athletically. Riding an extremely bulky horse is like driving a Mack truck in place of a Camero or a Porsche. At the other extreme is the horse that has muscles that are too slight. He will not have the muscle or power needed to perform and he is also more prone to injury. A slight gaskin muscle will make it hard for him to hold a slide or a spin or rollback.

Example of a good loin.

Loin

A strong loin combined with a long hip with a good slope to the hip helps a horse curl his hind legs under him as he slides to a stop. A horse's loin connects the thoracic cavity, or the barrel of the horse, to the powerful muscles of his hindquarters. A horse's loin is sometimes called the coupling. The loin transmits the power of the hindquarters to the forequarters of the horse. The loin must be strong, wide, and heavily muscled. A horse with a weak loin lacks the power and drive of a better built horse.

Hip

A horse with a good length and angle of hip allows him to bring his hind legs underneath his body as he lopes or spins or slides to a stop. By reaching further underneath himself with his hind legs, a horse will be able to elevate his front end to prepare to stop, to reach under and change leads hind end first (as is desirable), and to be in position to do whatever you might ask of him. A horse's hind hooves should reach close

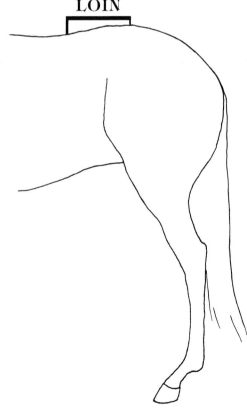

The loin transmits the power of the hindquarters to the forequarters as the horse moves.

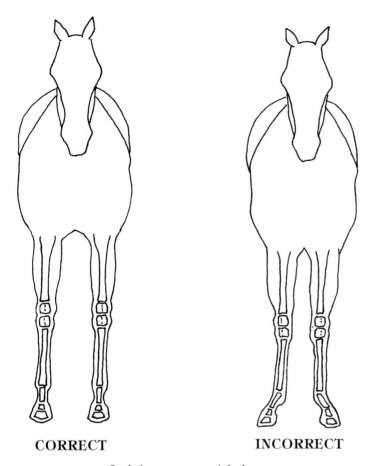

CORRECT   INCORRECT

Look for correct, straight legs.

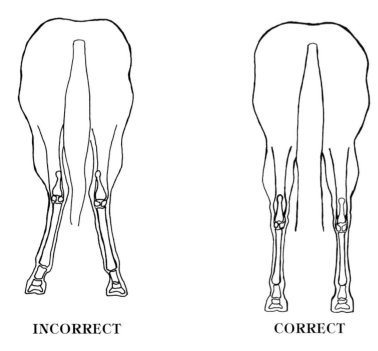

INCORRECT   CORRECT

The hind legs should be straight.

to the tracks made by his front hooves. A horse with hind legs that extend straight down and then push out behind his tail to move himself forward will have difficulty not only with changing leads and stopping, but with any maneuver that you might ask of him.

Straight Legs

Look for correct, straight legs that do not deviate from a straight-line (forward) path when in motion. The bones of the legs and the hooves of both the front and hind legs should be straight, toeing neither in nor out. However, a colt that toes out that has not yet fully developed may only need more time to mature. Often, a colt that toes out slightly will straighten out as he matures. As he matures and strengthens, his muscles will "pull" his front legs in into the correct position.

An older horse whose legs deviate from the correct, straight-line position uses too much energy as he paddles or wings his legs about in the air (prior to landing on the ground), as compared with a straighter-legged horse. Straight legs prevent the problems associated with crooked legs that cause unsoundness. A horse that toes out can hit the inside of his opposite leg as he swings his leg to the inside before moving it forward. A horse that toes out behind will "spread eagle" when he slides to a stop. This can cause soreness and may make him hesitant to stop hard the next time. *Minor* deviations can sometimes be helped by corrective shoeing, but they may still put additional stress on a horse.

Look for a horse that is a good mover and that moves fluidly. A horse that paddles or wings is wasting a lot of unnecessary movement. As is true of so many things, the most efficient way to perform is generally the quickest and uses the least amount of energy, energy that could be spent improving other areas of a maneuver.

Choose your farrier with care. Select one that works with your breed and discipline, and check references. (Farrier Don Truskauskas, the author's son, Harwinton, Connecticut)

Proper farrier work can keep your colt's legs straight. Start young and keep the feet and legs straight with correct trimming or corrective shoeing if needed. Notice the straight legs and correct conformation of this colt. Only time will tell if he has the mind to go with the body.

Hooves/Feet

A horse needs good, strong hooves that are able to hold a shoe without cracking or splitting or tearing off. Reiners are shod with sliding plates on the hind feet to enable them to perform the sliding stops that you see. Without a hoof to hold the shoe, his slides, as well as the rest of his performance, will be limited. The old saying of "No hoof, no horse," is still true today, especially when dealing with an athlete.

The size of a horse's hoof should be in relation to that of his body. Different breeds of horses also have slightly dif-ferently shaped feet and/or are shod slightly differently. Trying to shoe a Thoroughbred "stood up" like a Quarter Horse will make the Thoroughbred uncomfortable and quite possibly lame after a period of time. Shoeing a Quarter Horse like a Thoroughbred will also create problems. Choose a farrier who is qualified to shoe your breed or type of horse. Check on his references if there is any doubt in your mind. Often asking your vet his opinion can give you answers.

Given enough time, a good farrier can fix many shoeing or hoof problems. If you are looking to buy a horse, find a reputable farrier and ask him to look at the feet of the horse that you are considering. He may notice such things as contracted heels, white line disease, or thin walls that won't hold a shoe well—just some of the problems an un-trained eye may not pick up. Some

*Joe Ferro says
Splash has the
conformation
of a reiner.*

horses with "soft" feet may test as being lame when in fact all they need is a good set of shoes that are changed or reset every four to six weeks. Your farrier (and your vet) are very important people for you to know in the years to come. It is best to develop a good relationship with them and cultivate it over the years. Pay your bills promptly, be courteous, and listen to what they have to say. The best advice in the world will not help your horse if you do not put the time into following through with whatever treatment is prescribed.

AND FINALLY, WILL HE DO IT?

One of the most important things to remember is that the best-looking horse with terrific conformation will not win if he is not trainable. A good mind can overcome some conformation problems to a degree, if you use care, do not stress the horse more than is necessary, and accept his limitations. Yet if a horse fights you every step of the way, does not retain what he is taught, or is so "hot" that he cannot accept the training procedures, you can spend your entire life trying to train him and never succeed.

SIGNS OF A GOOD HORSEMAN

A good horseman is one who knows when a horse is not suited to the job at hand, either because of conformation (or lack of it) or because of his "mind." Sometimes people find it very hard to "give up" on a horse, accept his limitations, and go out and find a more suitable animal. *Some horses are not meant to be what you want them to be,*

When a horse is correctly balanced, you should be able to visually cut him in thirds. This horse's front is bigger than his middle, which is bigger than his hind end. He will not have the power nor the balance so needed to perform athletically. A balanced horse will stay sound and be able to perform with ease. Color is a bonus!

and no amount of wishing or training or praying will change them. That is something that you must learn to accept—it is not a reflection on you.

If all horses had the mind, the conformation, and the ability to be World Champions, riding one horse would be just like riding all the others. Just as some people are better suited at one job than another, some horses may or may not excel at a given discipline.

Horses have limitations just as people do. Accept them and find what the horse *could* be good for.

A horse that gets tangled up in his own legs is not a good reining prospect. Look for balance and athletic ability.

CHAPTER TWO

Training One Step at a Time

BUILD A FOUNDATION

Training a horse is similar to building a house—you must build a solid foundation. This foundation is what keeps the house—whether a ranch, colonial, or log cabin—standing day after day, year after year, storm after storm. When the foundation is built, you can begin to build the frame and then add rooms. With a solid foundation of training on a horse, you can go back to any point in your training program whenever the horse seems confused by a new step that you have introduced. You can add "rooms" to his foundation, teaching him to spin, to roll back, to slide to a stop, in the case of a reining horse. For a jumping horse, you would begin with work on cavellettis and then eventually vertical fences and oxers.

When you pay the foundation men for the work on your house, you trust that they have done a good job that will last for the life of your house. A horse's solid foundation is also built upon trust, although in a different way. The horse learns to trust you and know that you will not ask more of him than he is capable of giving. He trusts that you will not put him in a situation that will hurt him. He trusts that you will praise him and release all pressure when he is right (to show him that he performed the correct response). And he trusts that you will correct him humanely when he is wrong, then show him what is right so that he can avoid the same correction the next time.

Praise your horse when he is right.

BE CONSISTENT

Consistency is the key to training a horse. The more consistent your cues are, the faster the horse will learn. The actual cue itself does not matter—it is the *consistent* use of a cue that teaches a horse what to do. You must learn to break each training segment down into small sections and build one step at a time. You must reward the horse for each small attempt that he makes. These rewards tell your horse that he is on the correct path and that he understands what you have asked. The initial small attempts will lead to bigger and better responses to your given cue or signal. Rewarding the horse for a small attempt will make him want to try again the next time so that you will continue to reward him.

THINK ABOUT WHAT YOU ARE SAYING

Think about what you are telling your horse. Think about what you told

You reward your horse when he performs correctly by releasing pressure.

him yesterday, and be sure that today's lesson is consistent with that. You cannot let him perform one way today and change the rules tomorrow. Start slowly and easily. Reward your horse when he is right by the release of pressure. Correct him when he is wrong. Use your aids consistently so that the horse can learn this new, nonverbal communication system. For example, teach him that left-heel pressure always means a right-lead lope. To teach him this, you must consistently use that left-heel cue for a right-lead lope. However, if you let him lope on the left lead when you have given him the cue for a right lead and do not correct him, how is he to learn that there is a specific cue for each lead?

After you teach a horse what the different aids or cues mean, you will have the tools or aids to correct each part of his body.

FEEL WHAT YOUR HORSE IS SAYING

Before you can correct a horse, however, you must be able to *feel* that the horse is wrong. A horse must be straight and balanced to change leads and stop correctly. He must be upright, with his body aligned from head to tail to stop correctly. If a horse is loping circles and drops his shoulder into the circle, it will feel like you are cornering on a fast-moving motorcycle. He will not be upright and balanced to perform the next maneuver that you ask of him. But, if you cannot *feel* that the horse has dropped his shoulder, how will you know that you *should* correct him? You must be able to feel that his shoulder has dropped so that you can lift his shoulder before asking him to continue with the next maneuver. Lift your rein on the side of the dropped shoulder to lift the horse's shoulder so that he is upright and balanced before asking for a new maneuver.

If you let your horse lope on the wrong lead, how is he to learn that he must take the correct lead? You have to know when your horse is right so that you can leave him alone, and you must know when he is wrong so that you can correct him.

LEARN TO CORRECT YOUR HORSE

Even if you could bring your horse to a trainer for every problem that you ever have with the horse, the horse will soon figure out that you yourself do not have the knowledge or the ability to fix him if you continue to let him misbehave. Therefore, he may not be a problem to the trainer, but he will try his tricks on you time and time again until *you* learn when he is wrong and how to fix him.

COMMON TRAINING ERRORS

There are a number of common training errors that I see over and over as I work with novice trainers.

Waiting Too Long to Correct a Horse

A horse takes a wrong lead, but rather than immediately pulling him back to a walk and immediately asking him to lope on the correct lead, you either let the horse lope halfway around the arena before correcting him or stop the horse and sit on his back, frustrated. With the second option, the horse is actually enjoying the rest and has more incentive to take the wrong lead. Learn to think of how a horse *may* interpret your actions.

Beware of giving aids that are accidental.

Following a Prescribed Plan, Rather Than Reacting to How the Horse Performed This Time

While training, you must keep the larger goal in mind. For example, say that you have four cones set in a row as you might find in a horsemanship pattern. At the first cone, your plan is to walk, at the second, to jog, at the third, to lope, and at the fourth, to halt. Usually all goes well until the third cone. The horse is late in departing into a lope and so barely lopes a stride and a half before reaching the fourth cone. You pull the horse to a halt because you had planned to halt at the fourth cone.

The horse has just begun to lope and yet you are already pulling him back to a halt. Was he wrong to lope? That is what the horse will think. Because this is training and not a show, is it really that important that the horse halt at the fourth cone this time? Did the horse know that he was supposed to stop at the fourth cone? Wouldn't it have been better to allow the horse to lope and ask

Let the horse lope and ask him to halt at another point.

him to halt at another point? While training, you must keep the larger goal in mind. Forget the cones, and go with what the horse tells you.

Not Allowing the Horse to Make Mistakes

Some horses would rather walk to the inside or even across the arena rather than stay on the rail. While you can correct your horse by using either your leg or your rein to put him back on the rail, this becomes monotonous if the horse tries it repeatedly. It is a constant battle of wills, and the horse must learn not to keep trying. The answer is to let the horse begin to cut across the arena so that he will understand why he is being corrected. Immediately take your outside rein and pull the horse into small circles to the outside, or in the opposite direction from which your horse chose to go. Sometimes you must allow the horse to begin to make a mistake so that you can correct him and show him it is to his benefit not to make that same mistake again.

Not Praising Your Horse When He Is Right

Your horse has been unwilling to pick up his right lead and you have consistently brought him back to a walk to ask him immediately to lope again. Finally, one day, he takes the right lead but begins to lope too fast. Rather than getting after him for loping too fast and pulling on the reins to slow him down, which he could interpret as a correction, you must forget speed at this point in his training. Instead, praise your horse for taking the right lead. Sit quietly with your reins loose and let him lope. Let him understand that he performed correctly by letting him lope. When you are ready to ask him to slow back to a walk so that you can ask for another lope departure, use your body and your reins gently to ask him to slow down softly and quietly. Don't jerk or pull on his mouth to tell him to slow down. You can teach him to go slow later, after he has learned to take the correct lead. You must look at the long-term benefit—a horse that takes the correct lead.

BE PREPARED

A horse may get away with something once by surprising you; he may even do it twice. But the third time, you *must* be prepared to correct him. It is now a habit! If you are unsure how to correct your horse, do not put him in a position to perform the same sneaky maneuver before you have learned how to correct him. If your horse bucks when you ask him to lope, do not ask him to lope until you have a plan in mind to correct him. If you ask your horse to spin and he turns on his forehand (around his front legs), rather than on his haunches (or hind end) as is correct, do not ask him to spin again until you know how to correct him. If your horse runs out a gate every time you walk by it, have a plan in mind to correct him. Do not give your horse the opportunity to perform or learn a new bad habit. Decide on a corrective plan *before* your horse reaches the spot where he misbehaves or before you ask for the maneuver that requires correcting. Think ahead.

THINK BEFORE YOU TRAIN

Training is more of a mental endeavor than many people realize. It takes time to analyze what a horse has done wrong and then time to devise a game plan to correct him. Sometimes avoiding a particular area and returning to something that a horse does well—even as simple as walking or jogging in circles—and then returning to the problem area later is all it takes. Perhaps the horse was having an off day, or maybe he wasn't feeling quite up to par.

To train a horse, you must first talk to him in his language. Then you must think like him and understand how he interprets what you tell him. A correction, such as getting pulled into a tight circle, tells the horse that he was wrong and that he should avoid the behavior that caused him to get corrected. A reward, such as when you release all cues and sit relaxed on his back, tells him that he was right, and that he will want to repeat that behavior in the future.

The only way we have to talk to a horse is through the use of aids. You must be sure not to use an aid accidentally. For example, if your legs bounce on the horse's sides, how can he decipher which bump is an aid that he should obey, and which is one that he should ignore? If you poke him with a spur when you ask him to change leads, and he speeds up or kicks out, or begins to fear the lead change and tries

Make your horse circle if he tries to run out the gate. Make him work much harder when he is wrong than when he is right. Here, I've locked my left hand on my hip to make him circle.

to rush through it, you must understand why he performed as he did. Think back to why or how the problem started. Rider error causes many problems that are often blamed on the horse. Sometimes, you mistakenly or unknowingly cue the horse and then get angry at him. You must learn to control every part of your body so that you know what you are "saying" to the horse at all times.

The longer you ride, the more control you will gain over the different parts of your body. You must be able to sit balanced in the saddle; your weight should not shift around and throw the horse off-balance. Learn to use each hand independently from the other hand and also independently from each leg. Using an aid only when you want to "talk" to a horse or tell him to change that which he is doing is a key to successful training. When the horse

Talking to your horse in his language means understanding how he will interpret what you tell him.

is performing as he should, *sit quietly and leave him alone.*

Some basic thoughts to keep in mind when training are:

- Move your seat, legs, and/or hands only to tell the horse to change.
- Don't signal a change unless you want a change (beware of giving the horse extra cues without meaning to).
- Sit quietly if the horse is doing what you asked—this tells him that he is correct.
- Be consistent in your aids. By repeating your cues in the same way, the horse will know what is expected of him. The horse will understand, after a period of time, that if the left rein is pulled, he should follow his nose and go left.
- Be careful not to give aids that are accidental, such as pulling on the reins for balance or bumping with your legs if you do not mean to speed up or move away from pressure.
- Think of every move you make as telling the horse something.

USE AIDS OR CUES EFFECTIVELY

Since this is how you communicate with your horse, make sure you are consistent in your aids, rewards, and corrections. Let the horse know that he will be rewarded for doing as you ask, and let him know that he will be corrected if he is wrong. Every time you use your weight, reins, or legs, think about what you are telling the horse. Have you rewarded or corrected him?

Know your horse. Is he a hot-blooded Thoroughbred? Use a light correction and increase it slowly. Is he cold-blooded? You may want to carry a crop or use spurs to get his attention. Fit the strength of the cue or correction to the temperament of the horse. Training a horse is work. You must be aware at all times what you are telling him. You cannot goof off one day and forget to correct him, then overcompensate the next day for the same mistake. You have to know what is acceptable behavior and what is not and correct accordingly.

You must be able to step back and think about how *you* may have caused the problem. Did you hook him with a spur or bump him when he did nothing wrong? Did you catch his mouth without meaning to? Did you reward him for doing what you asked in order to tell him that he was right?

Change the horse's mind occasionally by doing nothing more strenuous than walking for an entire lesson. Work on the different suppling maneuvers. Go for a trail ride. Keep the horse quiet and relaxed. Let him enjoy his work so that he will try his best for you. Let the horse know that riding can be an enjoyable experience. Use lighter and lighter cues until your horse seems to move freely with no visible cues from you. Think like a horse, then talk to him in a language that he understands.

Watch your horse as he moves freely through the pasture, and think about how you can tell him to act that way under saddle. Then ride, ride, ride. Learn to sit quietly and to sit balanced. Use your aids softly and gently. Be consistent in your cues, rewards, and corrections. Make it easy for the horse to perform. The more hours you spend in the saddle, the closer you will get to your horse and what you once had to think about carefully will become second nature.

CHAPTER THREE

Ground Training

TRAINING BEGINS ON THE GROUND

Teaching a horse to longe and to obey your cues on the ground will also help when you ride that same horse. I use a round pen to teach a horse that he must obey the word "whoa!" and also to teach the specific cues to jog and to lope. I teach a horse that a "cluck" means to jog and a "kiss" means to lope. When I want a horse to increase his speed, such as when I want the horse to gallop (for his large, fast circles), I continue to kiss after he picks up the lope. Because he has learned to lope from the kiss, or to move on or go faster when I kiss, he understands to extend his gait to a gallop when you continue to kiss after he lopes.

Respect starts on the ground and carries over to work under saddle. A horse must respect you before he will obey you. Respect does not mean that a horse fears you; *fear* is a strong emotion that carries a negative connotation and the expectation of danger or harm. *Respect* means that one is submitting to or yielding to the heightened opinion of another, honoring that person's greater knowledge or ability.

Set the Stage for Future Training

This initial training on the ground sets the tone for the balance of your horse's training sessions. It makes a horse more respectful of you and your cues. Telling a horse that he responded correctly is important. It shows him that he can avoid the snap of the chain by obeying the verbal whoa command and can avoid the snap of the whip if he obeys the cues to go faster. He learns that you will reward him when he obeys correctly and correct him when he is wrong.

I start by longeing a horse for ten minutes and work my way up to twenty minutes. That is about the length of a young horse's attention span and is enough work on the ground to put most horses in a working frame of mind. You don't want to work a horse so hard that he is exhausted and too tired to learn anything by the time you get on his back. I use front splint boots. They give a horse support and can keep him from being injured if he plays in the round pen.

Early on, I teach my horses that the word "quit," said in a low tone of voice, means that they *have done* or *are doing*

Respect on the ground carries over to work under saddle.

the words when a horse is unsure of a new behavior, when he takes the first tentative crossover step as you teach the spin or takes his first steps backwards. Remember to keep your voice soft and your actions slow and quiet or you will scare him more than help him. The timing of your praise and corrections are essential as is the consistency of your rewards and corrections. You have three seconds to correct or reward a horse for him to associate that same correction/reward with his behavior.

> **You have three seconds to correct or reward a horse for him to associate that same correction/ reward with his behavior.**

Respect starts on the ground and carries over to work under saddle.

something wrong; they should change that behavior. I use a long, drawn out, "Good Boy/Girl" to tell my horses that I am pleased and that they will get rewarded. Their reward may be the release of pressure alone or in conjunction with a few minutes of rest. Horses seem to learn these words quite easily. I use the word "Quit" rather than "No" as "No" sounds too much like "Whoa!" I *never* want a horse to confuse those two words. Horses learn quite early in life to obey a threatening look or gesture—pinned ears, bared teeth, a hind end turned in their direction—from their dam and from other horses. They seem to pick up on the word "Quit" as my "threat" to them, similar to pinning my ears back.

They learn "Good Boy/Girl" almost as easily. Initially, you must say the words while you reward the horse. Once the horse understands that those words mean that he is correct, you can then use

Consistency

Consistency is a key to successful training and it is definitely critical in teaching a horse to obey your free longeing commands. I use a cluck for a jog and a kiss for a lope. I say "Walk" when I want the horse to walk and the word "Easy" when I want the horse to slow in a given gait. While you may change the words to suit yourself, using the same cues each time is extremely important.

Most horses learn free longeing easily if you have been consistent in your cues while longeing. The horse benefits from free longeing by being allowed to move in a natural position. When free longeing in the round pen, the horse's head and neck are not cocked to the inside, as can happen with a longe line. This allows the horse to carry himself straighter with his weight more evenly balanced. When you begin to teach a horse to give to the bit as discussed in the chapter on bitting, it is easier to free longe than to be encumbered by the additional longe line.

Respect for Your Commands

Teaching a horse that he must obey your command in one situation will carry over and help you in other situations. Teaching a horse to stand still for you to pick up his feet will also help when you ask him to stand to be saddled or clipped or mounted. Teaching a horse to lead and to go forward on your command (on the ground) will teach him he must obey your command to go forward under saddle.

You must show a horse what is acceptable behavior in this partnership and what is not acceptable behavior. It is not acceptable for a horse to bite, kick, or rear and strike at people. It is not acceptable for a horse to jog when you have asked him to lope or to gallop. And ignoring the whoa command is the biggest offense and is never acceptable.

ESTABLISHING FORWARD MOTION

You must read your horse and be sure not to ask for a change if he is not confident in his current frame of mind. You must enforce the whoa command, but do not ask him to stop if he has not established forward motion. In the early days of longeing, asking a horse to stop before he is relaxed and going forward (around your longeing circle) will only confuse him. Snapping the longe line to tell him to halt *before he is going forward confidently* may cause him to think that he should not go forward at all. You will see the look of confusion on the horse's face, and the resulting hesitation on his next attempt to go forward. *Read your horse and ask for a transition only when the horse is ready.*

TRAINING ON A LONGE LINE

If you do not have a round pen, you can longe a horse on a longe line

Be sure to establish forward motion.

and still get the benefits of this work. Whether free longeing or using a longe line, use this longeing time to *train* your horse. While longeing will rid a horse of excess energy, your horse will benefit more from his time in the round pen or on a longe line if you also use longeing as a training aid. Teaching your horse to obey your specific cues to walk, jog, lope, and halt on the ground will help later when you ride him. Longeing an older, spoiled horse can "remind" him to be respectful of your cues. An older, spoiled horse that bucks when asked to lope (these horses will figure out that bucking scares you and then you either won't ride or won't ask them to lope) will benefit by being made to lope from your cue on the ground. This will often teach one to lope under saddle without bucking. An older horse that has had time off due to a sickness or an injury can be brought back to condition while you are also teaching new commands or reinforcing old ones. Training a horse in the round pen can allow a horse to learn certain segments of the training program faster. A horse that is not encumbered by the weight and sometimes inconsistent aids of a rider can more readily understand such things as giving to the bit or learning the specific cues to jog and to lope.

Before asking any horse to move off in a longeing circle, first spend a few minutes rubbing the longe whip over his entire body. The horse must understand that the whip is an aid. It is not something to be punished with or something to fear. Spend as much time as necessary rubbing the whip over the horse's body until he accepts it as a training aid. Rub the whip along his sides, over his rump, up and down his neck and along his legs. Never put yourself in a position that is unsafe where the horse could kick at you or strike at you

with a front leg. Stay on the *side* of the horse and keep control of his head. Talk quietly while you rub the whip gently on his neck, hindquarters, and legs. Once he accepts this new training aid, progress to longeing.

To longe a horse to the left, hold the longe line in your left hand with the whip in your right hand. If you drew an imaginary line from your right hand to his rump and your left hand to his head, it would make a "V." Reverse the longe line and whip to go in the opposite direction. If you are free longeing the horse, your position will be the same, although you will not have a line attached to the horse's head. Standing in the wrong position is the reason for most failed longeing attempts. If you stand in line with the horse's shoulder, you will block his forward movement with your body position or your body language. Standing farther back, slightly behind where the stirrup hangs, will encourage a horse to go forward.

Start by asking the horse to walk as you gently swish the whip on the ground or tap his hindquarters with the whip to tell him to move forward. He may jog or lope, rather than walk. That is perfectly acceptable in the beginning days of training. Take your time and show the horse what you want. Be patient.

When the horse starts to walk, immediately cease all go-forward cues and let him walk around and follow the rail. Insist that he continue in the same direction. Many horses will think that longeing is a game. They will begin to duck back into the fence and go happily in the other direction until they become bored and switch directions again. Don't let them play this game. Watch your horse's ears. Most will flick an ear before changing directions. This is when you must be prepared and give an additional go-forward cue if your horse should think about switching directions. Make him turn back and go in the original direction if he does change directions. You must be in charge and tell him when to change directions—he does not get to choose.

When the horse understands to go forward, begin to teach the various cues, such as "Whoa!", a cluck for a jog, and a kiss for a lope. By using these cues consistently, the horse will understand these cues not only when free longeing, but when you ride him as well. To ask the horse to jog, cluck first. If he does not respond, snap the whip behind him to tell him to jog. Fit your cues to the horse. If he is very responsive, a swish on the ground may be enough to make him jog. If he is a quiet horse, a loud snap from the whip behind him may be necessary. Enforce the cue if necessary so that the horse learns from the beginning that he must respect your cues *and go forward on command.*

The Whoa Command

Every horse should be taught to stop immediately and to freeze when he hears the word "Whoa!" This is your safety word throughout a horse's training and it is also the beginning of teaching a horse to slide to a stop. When I stop a horse in the round pen, I want him to stop immediately. I do not want him to turn and face me. He cannot learn to slide to a stop if he turns. Re-inforce your whoa command as needed by using a chain under the horse's nose. Most horses learn quickly that they can avoid the snap of the chain by obeying the verbal command. *As soon as the horse stops, immediately* praise him. Every time a horse halts during his initial training, walk up to him slowly to rub his neck to praise him. You can scare a horse through your body language by rushing up to him. He might perceive your rushing as a threat. Walk up slowly and praise him with your voice as you

Notice my position when using a longe line. I stand in line with the stirrup, the whip behind the horse.

Once a horse longes well consistently, the whip may not be neccesary.

Most failed longeing attempts are caused by the handler stepping in front of the stirrup.

approach. Let the horse stand for a moment to enjoy his reward of a rest.

After a week or so, when the horse readily obeys your command to stop, you no longer need to approach the horse to praise him every time that he stops. A brief hesitation or a verbal "Good Boy/Girl" is sufficient. However, do let the horse stand for a moment so that he understands that he was correct in stopping. Rushing a horse to perform another gait or maneuver right after stopping can make him wonder if he was correct in stopping. Give him a moment to absorb the cue and the reward. At the other extreme is the person who continues to approach and pet the horse for every stop that the horse makes for weeks and weeks. Carried to this extreme, a horse will *expect* his reward and will not move until you pet him. You will have taught him that when he hears the word "Whoa!" he should be petted.

Ignoring the whoa command is *never* acceptable.

Remember that horses are creatures of habit. You must show them what you expect, but beware of creating a bad habit by overdoing the praise. Most horses truly want to please you, yet you must be sure to demand respect. If a horse does not respect you, he will do whatever is easiest for him to do. When a horse respects you, he will do his best to obey your commands—if he understands what it is that you want. For that reason, your commands must be clear to the horse.

When I say "Whoa!" and give a horse that first sharp tug or two on the longe line, most horses stop and look at me in utter surprise. They seem to wonder how I made them stop. I am still standing in the center of the round pen. Many horses will flick an ear back and forth after stopping, almost as if

questioning, "Was I right? Did I do good? Did I do the right thing by stopping?" Letting a horse stand after he stops is an easy answer to his question. Obviously he was correct in stopping as I have ceased all cues and/or pressure and allowed him to rest. Making a horse stop also shows the horse that I can control him from a distance. He learns that it to his benefit to obey my commands.

Occasionally, a horse will continue to run around the round pen after I say "Whoa!" or snap the longe line to enforce my command. This does not often happen if you have taught the horse to understand and respect your whoa command when you are leading him. Yet if a horse does not stop, it means first that the horse does not know what "Whoa!" means. He is running because he is afraid. Remember that horses have the flight response. They run from what they do not understand. Say "Whoa!" again and give a hard tug on the longe line. If necessary, pull his head to you, repeating the whoa command. If he still doesn't stop, you must decrease the size of the horse's circle until he has to stop, and then pull the horse's head to you. Say "Whoa!" *immediately* when he does stop. Then praise him and let him stand for a bit longer than normal the first time to show him that stopping was the correct response. Repeat this procedure until he fully understands the whoa command.

Horses that respect "Whoa!" on the longe line will usually stop from the same command when they are mounted. Using a verbal command as your horse learns will keep his mouth soft and responsive for later use. Never abuse the whoa command by saying "Whoa!" unless you *mean* "Whoa!" For safety reasons, this is the most important command that you can teach any horse.

Changing Pace

Let the horse go around the pen a couple of times until he is relaxed and moving freely. Only after he has made two to four circles should you ask for a transition to another gait. If you ask him to change gaits too soon, he may think that he is being corrected for doing something wrong. Giving him time to settle and relax at each gait will let him mentally absorb the cue. He will soon realize that you leave him alone when he responds correctly—the basis for all training. Only snap the whip when the horse needs to be told not to break gaits and to continue at his current speed or to increase his speed. Snapping the whip when the horse is performing correctly will only confuse him. *Your every action should tell him something. Your inaction means that he is performing as desired.*

To ask for a lope, make a kissing noise. Add the whip cue if he does not respond. Again, ask first, then "tell" him, and then enforce your command if necessary. If the horse lopes halfway around the pen and then breaks back to a jog, say "Jog" and cluck—the cue to jog. Do this as soon as he starts to jog. With much repetition, he will associate the word "jog" with slowing to a jog from a lope. Once he is moving in a relaxed manner at the jog, kiss to ask him to lope again. Make him lope for a couple of circles, then allow him to break to a jog or a walk. If he jogs, repeat the above-mentioned sequence of cues. If he walks, say "Walk."

It will take time for the horse to absorb these new cues. You must be consistent so that the horse will associate clucking with jogging and kissing with loping. At first, do not be overly concerned if the horse slows on his

In time your horse will associate a kiss with loping.

> Every action you make should tell your horse something. Inaction means he is performing correctly.

own if he is so inclined. Time your verbal commands with his breaking to a slower gait (or increasing to a faster gait). After two or three weeks, the horse should begin to respond more readily to your cues to increase or decrease his speed. Be sure that he will increase his speed from time to time when you ask him to do so. Never ask for a change of pace or stop him in front of the gate. You do not want him to think of the gate as a place to stop or as a way out. Also, never ask a horse to stop in a place where he has tried to stop before on his own. Make him wait for and respect your cues. When he halts correctly on your command at a point away from the gate, walk up to him, praise him, and then lead him across the pen and out. Reward good behavior, not bad behavior. Look for

Be sure to keep your whip behind the horse.

slight improvement when you are ending a lesson, keeping in mind that horses have a short attention span.

FREE LONGEING

After a horse obeys the whoa command in the round pen from your verbal command while longeing, remove the line and free longe the horse. If the horse does not stop from the verbal "Whoa!" *immediately* put the longe line back on with the chain under his chin. Send the horse around the pen a few times to establish his forward motion and then say "Whoa!" *with an accompanying snap* from the longe line. *Establishing forward motion is extremely important* before you ask the horse to halt. Don't confuse a horse by asking him to begin to travel around the first circle and then jerking him with the chain while yelling "Whoa!" The horse will wonder why he got the corrective

snap on his nose. Was it because he began to go forward, something that you had previously taught him was the correct thing to do? Or did he do something else wrong? Always establish forward motion before asking a horse to stop.

Changing Directions

To ask a horse to reverse when free longeing, stop him at a point away from the gate. Then step from your position to a point that is in line with his head. Use your longe whip as an extension of your arm. Place the whip in front of him and cluck to send him in the other direction. Then proceed with your cues to walk, jog, and lope in the opposite direction. Work both directions equally, or spend additional time on his stiffer or less obedient side. I much prefer to turn the horse in to the fence, *not* towards me. This helps him to get his butt under him and teaches the rollback.

CHAPTER FOUR

Bits and
Curb Chains

TRY IT ON FOR SIZE

Walking into your favorite tack store, you stand mesmerized before a wall of gleaming bits: silver, aluminum, and copper bits; curbs, rollers, snaffles, twisted wires, straight bars, shank bits. How do you choose? How do you know which is the right bit for your horse?

Your horse ultimately will let you know his preference in bits.

Ultimately, your horse will tell you which he prefers by his response—or lack thereof—to a particular bit. However, because your horse cannot talk, you must decide which bit to try first. This decision should be based on your horse's level of training and on the size of his mouth. Too large a mouthpiece fits sloppily in a horse's mouth, leaving too much room on either side; it also affects

the timing of your rein signals to a horse. A bit that is too small pinches the sides of a horse's mouth and can cause him to become cranky or resentful because of the discomfort. Aim for approximately one-eighth inch on either side of the mouthpiece—enough room for his lips

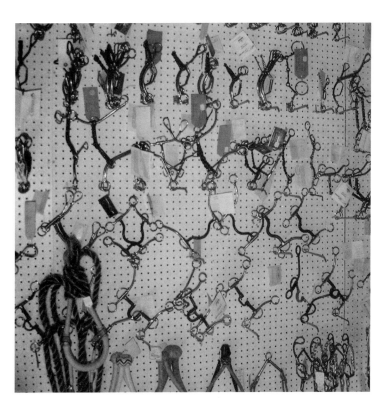

A wall of gleaming bits. How do you choose?

to fit comfortably around the outside edges of the bit.

You must also consider the thickness of the bit. Generally speaking, the thicker the mouthpiece, the milder the bit. However, if the horse cannot close his mouth around the bit easily, it will cause discomfort for the horse. Anytime a horse is uncomfortable, it will show in his attitude and affect his reaction to the signals given by the bit. While a horse may learn to tolerate carrying an uncomfortable bit in his mouth, you will lose the ability to communicate lightly and effectively with him.

> **Using a bit that is beyond a horse's level of training can scare him and set him back months in training.**

USE A SUITABLE BIT

Using a bit that is suitable for a horse's level of training is another important consideration. A bit is a cue—a signal to the horse—a way to tell him what you want, rather than a way to force him to respond. Using a bit that is beyond a horse's level of training can scare him, possibly setting him back months in training time. A horse must learn to *trust the signals* given by the bit, rather than to fear the pain that can be caused by it. Teaching a horse that he must respect the aids or signals given by the bit, as well as trust that the bit will not hurt him, is an ongoing process. Care must be taken to "talk" softly to your horse.

Start in a Snaffle

A colt should be started in a snaffle bit—a bit without shanks. This type of bit creates a direct line of communication from the rider to the horse via the reins. A snaffle allows you to teach a horse the rudimentary skills of rein signals or cues. Only after a horse has learned the true purpose of a bit should

Ring snaffle with a curb chain attached to keep the bit from being pulled through the horse's mouth.

he be advanced to a curb bit, or a bit with shanks and a curb chain.

Switch to a Curb Bit

When you switch to a curb bit, there is a brief hesitation or signal that comes through the bit (when the rider picks up the reins) before the bit actually "takes hold" of a horse's mouth. This signal, as it is called, allows the horse to prepare his next action before the bit takes effect if you move your hands slowly. It is this signal that allows a horse to stop long before the bit actually pulls on his mouth—if he has been carefully taught to respect and obey the signals that come from a bit.

A curb bit with reins loose.

When the reins are tightened on a curb bit (or shank bit) poll pressure is applied, as well as pressure from the curb strap.

With a well-trained horse, a slight lifting of the reins is all that is needed to bring him to a complete halt. A bit with a loose curb chain and short shanks allows a horse *more* time to prepare to react. A long-shanked bit with a tight curb chain gives him *less* time to react.

Another point to consider is the balance of the bit. Put the bit (minus the reins and headstall) on your finger and see where the bit balances naturally. If the shanks hang forward naturally, that is the position to which they will return once you release the reins. This type of bit allows the horse more reaction or signal time and allows him to carry his head slightly more forward than vertical. If the shanks hang straight down naturally, the bit will help to keep your horse's face more vertical, as is required in a Western Pleasure class. Your horse will learn to carry a bit where it balances most comfortably in his mouth. This is just one

more reason to choose the proper type of bit for your horse.

Check the Horse's Mouth

Before switching to any type of bit, or looking at a bit as the cause of a horse's problem, first open his mouth and check his teeth for proper wear and sharp edges. Wolf teeth—the small, pointed premolars located in the upper jaw—can interfere with a bit and cause a horse pain. Check for sharp edges on the back molars, or have your vet or an equine dentist check the horse's teeth to rule out a physical problem.

A snaffle bit forces the horse's cheeks against the edges of the upper premolars. If these teeth are sharp, a horse's cheeks can become bruised or lacerated. A horse's teeth should be floated, or rasped, with the sharp edges filed off once a year—more often if there is an unusual problem.

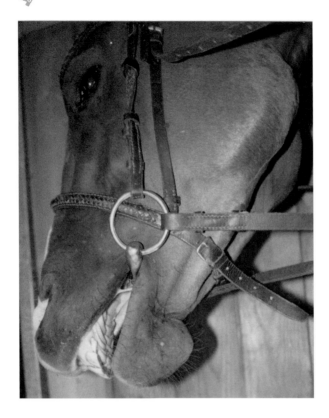

If a horse shows discomfort when bitted . . .

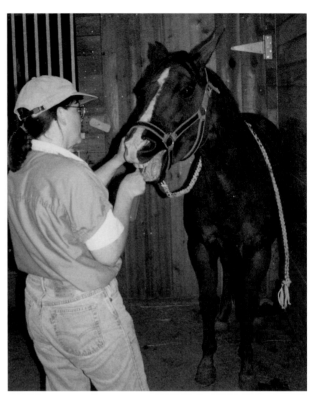

. . . have your equine dentist check his teeth. Many young horses have wolf teeth that must be removed!

Foam is a good thing! It tells you your horse's mouth is moist and responsive. A dry mouth indicates fear, just as our mouths get dry when we are scared.

Try It Out

Finding the best bit for your horse is often accomplished though trial and error. Choose a bit that fits your horse's mouth and one that you feel is suitable for his level of training. Then ride him in it for two to three weeks. Note the response he gives you. Will he respond to a light signal or cue? Or does he act as if he cannot "hear" what you are saying to him? Does he toss his head in the air as if he is uncomfortable or stick his nose in the air every time that you touch the reins? Is his mouth dry or moist? A relaxed, happy horse—one that is happy with his equipment and his job—will mouth a bit, making the saliva or foam that you see. A scared horse has a dry mouth. (This can be a reaction to fear in humans as well.) A scared horse will not "hear" you. His mind will be on his fear rather than on the signals that you are sending through the reins.

I start all colts in a thick, hollow-mouth eggbutt snaffle. Then I move on to a thinner, sweet-iron snaffle when the horses lose that light "feel" in the eggbutt snaffle. A thinner mouthpiece makes the bit slightly sharper, or more severe, so they continue to respect the bit.

If a colt is very tough-mouthed or begins to ignore the sweet-iron snaffle, I'll go to a single twisted-wire snaffle for a few days so that he begins to respect the bit again. Note: This type of bit can be severe in the wrong hands. Don't use it unless you have "good" hands.

Once a colt understands to neckrein and to flex at the poll, and generally understands the signals given by the bit, then I use a short-shank Mullen mouth bit. This helps make the transition to a curb bit, which later will allow me to ride one-handed.

After the transition period, I'll go to a slightly longer, five- to seven-inch shank with the same mouthpiece. Most horses like this bit; however, if a horse doesn't, then I begin to experiment with different bits to find what he *will* work in. Remember, you should always check his mouth and teeth for physical problems if a horse is showing signs of discomfort or seems unhappy with a bit.

Trying different bits over a period of time, especially if your horse is not responding as he should after you have checked all physical problems, is an acceptable method for finding the right bit. Don't assume that because your horse came with a specific bit, it is necessarily the proper bit for him.

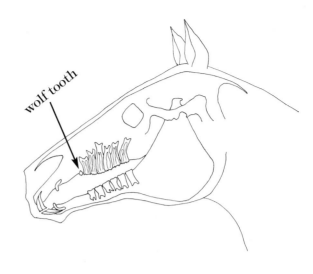

Wolf teeth are located as shown and must be removed. They are small and may be hard to see. Ask your vet if your horse seems uncomfortable in his mouth—most young horses have these teeth.

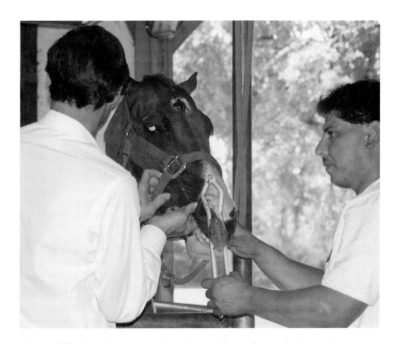

A qualified equine vet or dentist can float the teeth (removing sharp edges), remove wolf teeth in the young horse, and check for retained caps (baby teeth that didn't shed for one reason or another. (Dr. Ben Cornelius, Eustace, Texas)

When starting a colt, I use these bits: I start with the egg-butt snaffle on the left, and then I switch to a thinner, sweet-iron snaffle. If the horse is real heavy in my hands, then I go to a twisted-wire snaffle for a short time to teach him that he must respect the signals given by the bit.

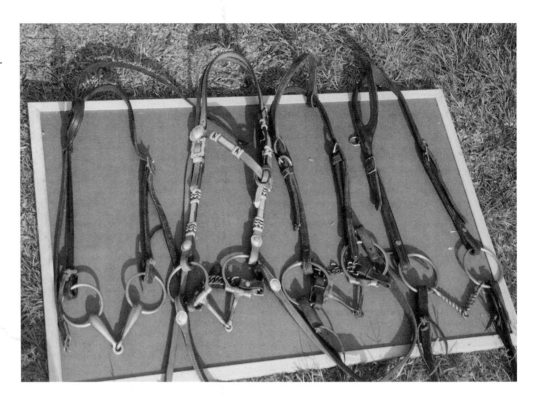

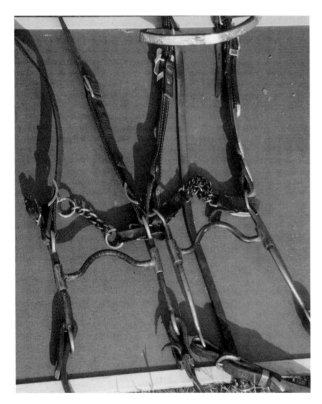

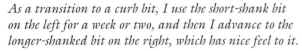

As a transition to a curb bit, I use the short-shank bit on the left for a week or two, and then I advance to the longer-shanked bit on the right, which has nice feel to it.

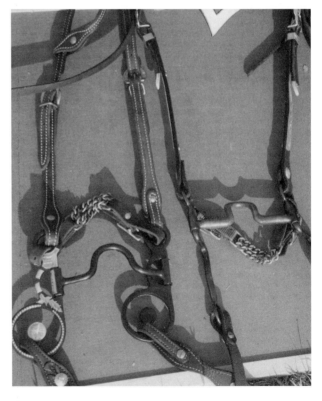

If I get an older horse in for retraining that doesn't respect the longer-shanked bit, I'll try one of these more severe bits—the one on the right being the most severe. When he learns to respect and obey the cues, I'll go back to a milder bit. Keeping a horse's mouth soft and responsive is the goal.

Always check his mouth and teeth for physical problems if your horse is showing signs of discomfort or seems unhappy with a bit.

Hang a bit in a horse's mouth and let him learn to carry it.

TEACHING THE COLT TO ACCEPT THE BIT

The first step in teaching a colt to accept a bit is to hang a bit in his mouth and let him carry it. A colt must first learn to adjust to the feel of this strange piece of metal in his mouth. He must become comfortable with that sensation before he can relax and understand the signals given by the bit. If you bump a colt's mouth—or any horse's—as you put in a bit or take one out, he will try to avoid being bitted the next time. The horse will see the bit and know that it will cause him pain. In self-defense, he will raise his head to avoid the whole procedure. Prevent this scenario by putting in a bit and taking it out with care. Do not let the bit drop and bump the horse's teeth. Go slow!

After teaching a colt to follow his nose in response to bit pressure by tying his head side to side, teach him to "give" to the bit, or to flex at the poll. He learns to drop his head to a vertical position to gain relief from bit pressure. In effect, he is backing off of the bit pressure. This is the opposite of a horse's natural response. An untrained horse will push into the bit, fighting pressure with pressure, rather than giving to pressure—the desired response. Giving to the bit is a procedure that takes months, not days or weeks, as you reprogram a horse to act in an acceptable manner.

The Mild Snaffle

To educate a horse in the use of a bit, begin with a mild snaffle. It will allow you to "pull" a horse or colt around without fear of hurting him. Generally, you must exaggerate your aids at first to show the horse what you want. If you start with a bit that is too harsh in the initial stages of training, your colt will learn to fear the bit and to fear the signals coming from it. You want him to understand and trust the signals coming from the bit. Only after he understands the signals given by a bit—i.e., turn left, right, and halt—can you go to a somewhat thinner mouthpiece to keep him somewhat respectful of the bit. A thinner mouthpiece will reinforce that the colt must obey the signals given by the bit. If a horse learns that he can ignore the signals of a bit, advancing to a slightly stronger bit can actually help to keep him light and responsive—if you have good hands.

The old saying, "The better your hands, the stronger (or harsher) the bit can be," is still true today. My definition of "good hands" is that you are able to feel a horse's response and use only as much pressure as necessary to get your point across. You can feel that the horse has responded, and you release all pressure when he does respond. You know when a horse needs a little less pressure to get your point across, and so you *use* less pressure. When he needs a little more pressure, you use more pressure, rather than using the same amount "because that is what you always use." Good hands also include knowing exactly when to use bit pressure to correct your horse or when to use legs, weight, or seat aids instead.

A rider with good hands can use a stronger bit. He knows exactly what signals he is sending the horse at all times and uses just enough pressure to get his point across. He consistently rewards the horse for a proper or correct response by releasing all pressure on the bit.

You may want to use a stronger bit if your horse has become somewhat deadened to the feel of a bit in his mouth or if he has lost respect for that bit. A stronger bit will remind him that it is always in his best interest to respect your aids when you give them. Then you can release the aids more quickly, making them look almost invisible. Sometimes, going to a stronger bit for a few days is all the reminder that a horse needs. Then you may go back to the original bit.

> **"Good hands" means having the ability to feel the horse's mouth through the reins and the ability to apply pressure when needed and a release when needed.**

Bits can be made of one solid piece or can have shanks that swivel or move independently of one another. A bit with longer shanks (the length from the mouthpiece to where your reins attach)

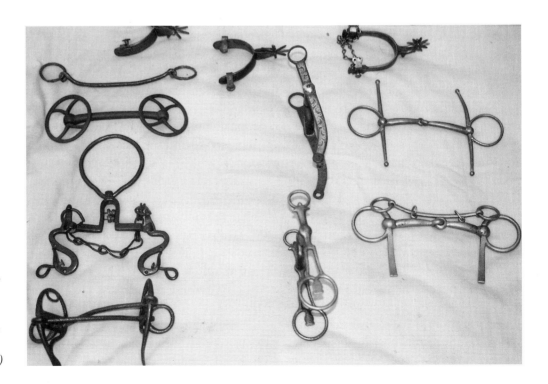

Examples of old bits. Look how far we have come. (These must have been torture for a horse whose rider had heavy hands!)

has more leverage, making this a stronger, or harsher, bit. A tighter curb strap will cause the action of the bit to occur sooner. However, two fingers under the curb chain is the accepted standard. Adjusting your curb chain this way allows the shanks to move one-half to two-thirds of the way back in response to pressure on the reins before the curb chain comes into play. As a horse becomes trained to obeying the signals given by a correctly used bit, he will start to obey as he feels the reins moving on his neck. Remember, the bit signals a horse—*it does not force* a horse to respond.

A bit with a high port—for example, a Spade bit—will push into the roof of a horse's mouth, making this an *extremely* harsh bit that should be used only by a trainer experienced with such bits. A straight bar is milder and rests on the horse's tongue, although a horse with a thick tongue may find this uncomfortable. A bit that has a slightly raised port provides tongue relief and is favored by many horses.

If you are a beginning rider or if you have not yet learned to feel whether you are using the bit to balance, do not be in a hurry to advance to a stronger bit. Balancing on a horse's mouth is a signal that a few lessons are in order to help you conquer this habit. You might be applying a bit aid more strongly or more often than is required. With a milder bit, there is less chance of doing serious harm to a horse's mouth. Any bit, however, can seriously harm a horse's mouth if it is used improperly. Ride in the mildest bit in which you have control of your horse—until you have complete control over your hands, legs, weight, and seat. *Do not balance by using the reins.*

A horse should be taught the basics of a bit before being moved to a stronger, more advanced bit. I always start a colt in a mild snaffle so as not to scare him. I want him to understand the concept of a bit before I move on to a stronger one. Many horses can be taught almost all they need to know in a snaffle. Then, when they understand, you can change to a curb or shank bit so that you can refine your aids to the lightest signal possible. Older horses must eventually switch to a shank bit for showing purposes. Making the switch to a shank bit and riding one-handed should not cause him undue distress if he has previously learned to understand the signals coming from the bit.

Snaffle bits are made to direct rein a horse—to pull his head in the direction in which you wish to go. Direct reining with a curb bit can send confusing signals to a horse. Stopping a horse with a snaffle bit pulls straight back on the corners of his mouth. Pulling on the corners of a horse's mouth causes less pain than pressure on the bars or gums of his mouth does. The reason an uneducated horse raises his head in the air when a rider pulls on the reins is because he is trying to put the bit pressure where he can best tolerate it. Also, a horse's natural response is to answer pressure with pressure. You pull and he pushes against the pressure.

A horse educated to the use of the bit through months of training is taught to "give" to the bit, or to flex at the poll. He learns that he is rewarded for giving to the bit and the pressure stops. However, if you never reward your horse for giving to the bit, he may revert to sticking his nose in the air just to avoid pressure.

A horse may become confused while learning to give to the bit. He may think that if tension on the reins means to flex at the poll, how can it mean to stop? This must be worked through, and the

Only after a horse understands what the signals from the bit really mean should you advance to a shank-type of bit.

horse must be taught that different signals from the bit can mean different things. It is a learning process. Only after a horse understands what the signals from the bit really mean should you advance to a shank-type of bit.

The Curb Bit

A loose-jawed (the shanks swivel independently)Mullen mouth bit (a bit with a slight rise in the mouthpiece that provides room for a horse's tongue and thus relieves the bit pressure on his tongue) with short shanks is what I often use to switch a colt from a snaffle to a curb bit. I personally like the feel of such a bit. Your horse will learn to feel for the movement of the bit before the curb chain comes into play (i.e., tightens under his jaw). The short shanks decrease the severity of this type of bit, allowing your horse to learn to trust the signals coming from the bit. Please note that, if your hands are heavy, this bit can still be quite severe because of the leverage, no matter how small the shanks.

Another option is the same type of bit, but one that has a broken or jointed mouthpiece. I personally do not care for this type of bit and only try it when I find that a colt is unhappy in other bits. I give him a chance to tell me if he is more comfortable in this type of bit. This sometimes happens because the jointed mouthpiece reminds him of the ring snaffle. What I dislike about these bits is that if you pull hard enough, the colt's mouth ends up being in a nutcracker situation. Because the shanks are jointed with the added leverage, the mouthpiece points to the top of the colt's mouth and the shanks add the squeeze—very similar to a nutcracker.

If a colt isn't happy in the Mullen mouth bit, I try a Billy Allen. The roller located in the center of the Billy Allen mouthpiece locks when the reins are pulled together, making it act much the same as the Mullen mouth bit for stopping, yet the independent action, due to that jointed roller, allows you to

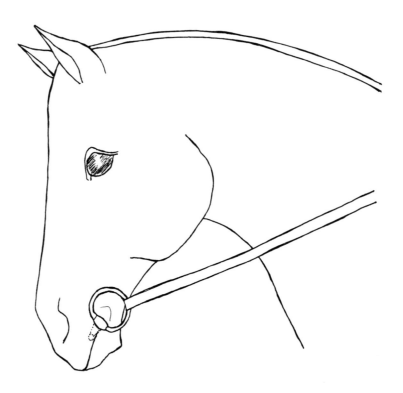

The snaffle bit pulls on the corners of a horse's mouth. Compare this to the curb bit pictured earlier.

influence one side of the colt at a time—for example, when he drops a shoulder. Some colts may not like this bit because it doesn't have the center rise to give relief from tongue pressure as does the Mullen mouth bit.

GOING TO THE NEXT STEP

If a colt ever begins to run through a bit, or needs a bit that is somewhat stronger to help him understand to flex at the poll and "give" me his face, I switch to a longer-shanked bit. If you do this, you must be extremely careful of the amount of pressure that you apply. Just as you learned in high school, the more leverage you have, the stronger you become. This is doubly important when applied to the bit, because it is in a horse's mouth, the most sensitive part of his body.

Another type of bit that I use from time to time is a one-piece or solid bit. The shanks do not move independently of each other; therefore, it is sometimes a good bit for a beginning rider who has trouble keeping his reins even as he learns to ride. A nervous or "hot" horse will sometimes play too much with a loose-jawed bit; switching to this solid bit sometimes seems to help.

DEMYSTIFYING THE CURB CHAIN

The curb chain (or strap) is the strip of chain (or leather) that attaches to the underside of a shank bit and lies under your horse's jaw. A curb *chain* is made of chain. A curb *strap* is made of leather. You will also find a combination of strap and chain—the leather attaches to your bit by a strap and buckle and then attaches to the chain that lies under your horse's jaw. This would

Many horses like this mouthpiece. The mild port in the middle does not push down on the horse's tongue and so gives a horse plenty of tongue relief.

be classified as a curb chain because it is the chain part that comes into play under the horse's jaw; the leather only buckles and holds it to the bit. The thinner the curb chain, the more "bite" it has, or the more severe it is. The NRHA rules state that curb chains are permissible but must be one-half inch in width. They must lie flat against the horse's jaw and must be free of barbs, wire, and twists.

What exactly does this curb strap or chain do? When used with a ring snaffle bit, it does nothing more than help keep the bit from being pulled through a colt's mouth. It does not change the effect of the snaffle bit in any way. It cannot make the snaffle bit more or less severe, because it does not affect the pull on the bit.

The ring snaffle, Dee-ring snaffle, and eggbutt snaffle are all bits that work off the corners of the horse's mouth. The various mouthpieces of these bits attach to the same rings to

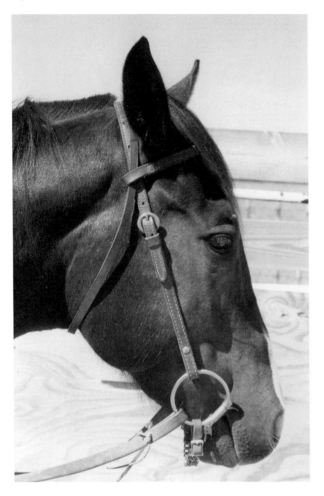

A curb chain on a snaffle bit does not increase the severity of the snaffle bit.

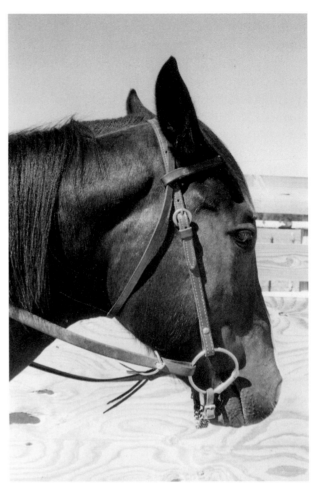

When the reins are pulled, the curb chain does nothing. I use it on a snaffle only to keep me from pulling the bit through his mouth.

which your reins attach. There is no leverage involved with this bit. When you pull the reins, the rings pull the mouthpiece directly back against the corners of the horse's mouth. The curb chain just hangs off the rings. It does not, and cannot, increase the severity of the bit. When the reins are pulled back, the curb strap does not change position from when the reins hang loosely.

I always add a curb strap to a snaffle bit when starting a colt. A green colt may open his mouth wide enough to allow the rings of the bit to slide right into his mouth while he is trying to learn, or perhaps trying to evade, the bit signals during early training. The curb

strap helps by making a loop with the bit around the colt's lower jaw so that the rings of the bit cannot get pulled into his mouth.

When a colt is switched to a shank bit—after he is educated to the bit by use of a snaffle—then the curb chain *will* enhance the action of the bit. When the reins are tightened, the shanks—the part of the bit from the mouthpiece to the bottom of the bit where the reins attach—move back in response to the pull of the reins. The ring at the top of the bit, or at the top of the purchase (the segment of the bit from the mouthpiece to the top of the bit), moves forward. The actual mouthpiece of the bit is the pivot point. Pulling on the reins moves the shanks back and the top of the purchase forward. The curb chain is attached to the top ring of the purchase. As that ring moves forward, the curb chain tightens, putting pressure under the horse's jaw. The headstall of the bridle is attached to the same ring to which the curb strap is attached, and so pressure is also applied to the top of the horse's poll by the downward pull on the headstall.

Obviously, using a very thin wire in place of a half-inch, flat chain will apply more pressure or pain under the horse's jaw. The same is true if you placed a barb or twist on the curb chain under the horse's jaw. When the reins are pulled, the barb or twist would dig up into the horse's lower jaw. Using a thin chain will increase the severity of a bit by causing pain under the horse's jaw. These types of curb straps are unacceptable for showing or any other purposes. They will cause a horse to raise his head to avoid the pain. This is the opposite of what you are trying to teach your horses.

The rule of thumb when adjusting a curb strap or chain is to allow two fingers between the chain and the horse's jaw. In other words, there should be enough slack in the curb chain when the reins are loose to allow you to insert two fingers between the horse's jaw and the curb chain. This gives the horse a chance to feel the slack come out of the reins. He can feel the action of the bit—and the resulting poll pressure caused by the purchase of the bit moving downward, tightening the headstall of the bridle—before the curb chain actually tightens on his jaw. The shanks of your bit should move back approximately one-half to two-thirds of the swing of the shank before the curb chain comes into play. A curb chain adjusted too tightly does not allow the horse to feel the signal of the bit moving before he is "grabbed" under the jaw by the curb chain. Using a curb chain properly allows the horse to feel the signal of the bit as it was meant to be felt. Used properly, it enhances the action of a bit.

Your hands—more than any bit, mouthpiece, shank, noseband, curb strap or chain—decide how harsh or light a bit is. Your horse will benefit if you think of the reins and the bit as a way to *signal* him to perform rather than a way to force him to perform. A horse stops because he knows that he will be rewarded and that the pressure will be released when he does stop.

The end result of training any horse is to have him respond to light, barely visible aids. This requires an ongoing commitment from you. Speak softly to your horse.

poll
pressure

curb chain
pressure

bit
swivels

As you pull the reins with a shank bit, the curb chain comes into play. Also, poll pressure is applied as the bit swivels.

CHAPTER FIVE

Teaching Your Horse to Accept Bit Pressure

THE BITTING PROCESS

A horse must be taught the proper way to respond to the bit. An untrained horse will fight pressure with pressure. This bitting process can begin before you ever get on a colt's back, or it can be taught in conjunction with training a horse under saddle. It can also be taught to an older horse that needs to learn how to respond properly to the bit.

To teach a horse how to "give" to the bit or to flex at the poll in response to rein pressure, start by tying his head first to one side and then to the other. Outfit your horse in a bridle with a snaffle bit and a saddle or surcingle on his back. Take him to your round pen or to any enclosed area free of obstacles. I prefer not to start in a stall on the chance that a horse may try to fight. A stall is too small and confining for the first few days of this training, although once the horse understands to give his head to pressure, you then can certainly tie his head in the manner described below in a stall. Most horses won't cause a problem, but I feel it best to start the first few days in a somewhat larger, enclosed area so that both you and the horse have room to move.

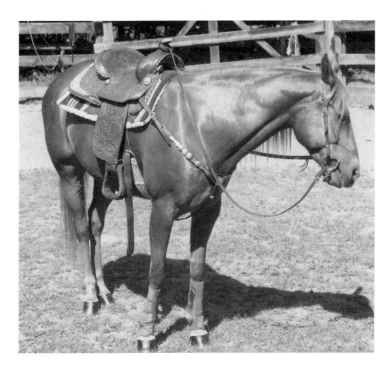

Tie one rein loosely to the saddle horn. Do this only with a snaffle bit!

Tie one rein loosely to the saddle horn, allowing the horse enough room to turn his head in the opposite direction comfortably. Take the opposite rein and ask the horse to bend his nose just slightly toward the saddle. Tie that rein to the girth where the skirt of the saddle ends. Once your horse is tied in this manner, cluck to him to ask him to "follow his

43

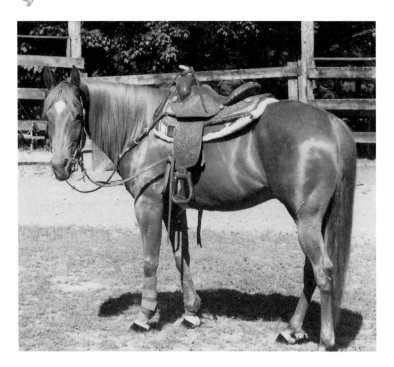

Take the opposite rein and tie it to the girth, bending the horse's head as shown.

as you did in the above step or using a running martingale.

Running Martingale

A running martingale has two rings which slide over the reins on each side (rather than just the one strap which attaches to the noseband as you would find on a standing martingale). You'll need eight-foot reins attached to a snaffle bit if you choose to use the running martingale. You should *only* use some sort of snaffle bit—a bit with no shanks. (Using either of these methods with the reins attached to the shank on a bit would put excessive pressure on the horse's mouth and can easily cause a horse to flip over).

Adjust and then tie the rings so that when the reins are attached to the bit, through the rings, they make a straight line to the saddle horn. To hold the rings in place, take a piece of twine or a strap, and tie one end to one ring. Put the twine over the horse's neck and tie it to the other ring, holding the rings in the same position so that the reins make a

Use a snaffle bit when beginning to teach your horse to bend at the poll.

nose" and to follow the arc of the circle in which he is tied. This teaches him that he must give to the one-sided pressure. Not only will he "follow his nose" and turn, he will begin to flex at the poll to gain relief from bit pressure.

The first two or three days, I ask him to follow the bend of the circle by clucking to him or by gently swishing a longe whip on the ground. Tie him for five to ten minutes on each side and ask him to circle. Then release him and go on to something else. As long as your horse is showing no signs of resentment—and he should not—then you may leave him tied on either side for fifteen to twenty minutes. Watch him the first few days until you are sure that he understands that to gain relief of pressure, he must follow his nose and bend or flex at the poll and give to the bit.

After two weeks of tying your horse in this manner, you may progress to the next step, which is either tying your reins directly to the girth of the saddle

straight line to the horse's mouth. Run the reins through the rings of the running martingale, proceed down between the horse's front legs, then tie the reins together up over the top of the saddle, behind the horse's front legs. When the horse begins to walk or trot, one shoulder will first bump one rein back and that same bump will be felt in the horse's mouth. You'll see the bit bump back in

To "set" a horse's head, you can tie the reins directly to the girth . . .

. . . or use the running martingale with the saddle . . .

the horse's mouth, first left, then right. When you later bump the horse's mouth with your reins, the feeling will be similar and he'll understand to drop his head to a vertical position.

Start Loose

The first couple of days are the most crucial. Start very loose, using only enough pressure on the reins so that if the horse sticks his nose in the air, he'll feel light pressure. Do not start a horse too tightly. He needs time to learn that the proper response is to drop his head to a vertical position or to flex at the poll to gain relief from bit pressure. This is not something that you can rush any horse through. Over a period of days, you'll see the bit bumping his mouth and the horse will drop his nose to a vertical position (bringing it back) in response to the pressure on the bit. Then you may tighten the reins a little every few days. *Tying a horse too tightly initially can cause him to panic and flip over backwards.* Start loosely! Send him forward with the whip if he fights.

Once the horse's head is tied in this way, you may either free longe him or use a longe line attached to his halter or

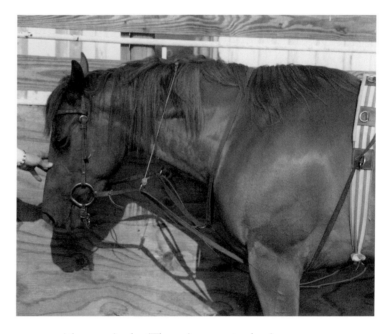

. . . or with a surcingle. (These rings are too low.)

a longeing cavesson. Ask the horse to move off in a longeing circle. The first time or two that he hits the bit, his head may come up and his hind end drop. He may try to stop and run backwards. In the worst scenario, he may rear and go over backwards. Use your longe whip, extended away from you so that you stay out of harm's way, and send the

Start loose (these rings are better) . . .

. . . and gradually increase tension.

horse forward with the whip. Do this aggressively enough so that the horse goes forward. Don't let him start running backwards. *Make him go forward* so that he'll realize that the way to release all pressure on his mouth is to drop his nose and go forward.

Know Your Horse

Know your horse. If he fights every little thing that you do, start very loosely, and *very* gradually tighten the pressure. If he's a calm, accepting type of horse, you can increase the pressure a

little sooner, *but only after a few days of his being tied very loosely.*

Once the horse is going around your longeing circle, ask him to walk, jog, or lope. You may ask him to halt and then repeat the process. Transitions are helpful in teaching the horse that his nose must stay vertical even when he changes pace. However, changing gaits too often or too quickly will confuse him. Let him change gaits and then go at least twice around the circle in a round pen before you ask for another transition. This gives him time to realize that he performed as you asked and time to learn to give to bit pressure and thus reward himself.

Increase Tension on the Reins Slowly

Once you see the horse's nose drop to a vertical position every time he hits the bit, you can begin to tighten up the reins a little more, until his face is vertical. Never tie a horse so tightly that his face is past vertical, because it will teach him to overflex. He'll then learn to tuck his nose into his chest and go behind the bit, leaving you with no control at all.

Continue to longe the horse this way for ten to twenty minutes, four or five times a week, before you ride. It usually takes about three months (possibly more) for a horse to really understand what you are asking—to give to the bit or to drop his nose to a vertical

> **Never tie a horse so tightly that his face is past vertical, because it will teach him to overflex.**

The rings on this running martingale are adjusted correctly. They only come into play if the horse raises her head. If you set them lower, the horse cannot transfer her weight to her hindquarters, which is always your goal. Make sure you work the horse in both directions, one side at a time.

Then longe her with her head set back to teach her to flex. (Here, the rings should have been higher on the horse on the left. They are correct on Magic on the right.)

position in response to bit pressure. This is called putting a "face" on a horse. You don't have to ride the horse every day. Longeing him with his head tied in this way will accomplish a lot, even without riding. Never let the horse stop when he is fighting the bit while being longed. Wait until he is flexing properly, or to the best of his ability at that time. Then say "Whoa," let the horse stop, and untie his head. Spend a few minutes letting him relax and catch his wind, and either ride him or put him away for the day.

The end result of this program is to have your horse carry his head in a vertical position. You can see the bumping action here.

When mounted, take a light, even contact with the reins and push your horse into the bridle with your legs—he should flex at the poll as shown.

RIDING THE HORSE

After the horse seems to understand, begin to ask him to give the bit while you are riding him. To accomplish this, let the horse walk or jog along the rail. It is easier for a horse to learn this at the jog or trot, because he naturally carries his head in a more vertical position. Once he is jogging, pick up light contact and take a light, even hold of the reins. Ask the horse to "give" his head to you and to flex at the poll. Hold your hands steady. Do not pull back on the reins. As you take hold of his face (or the reins), you must push or squeeze the horse up into the bridle with your legs. Your legs create the extra energy and your hands capture that same energy, causing the horse to flex at the poll as he drives from behind and rounds his back.

Having control of a horse's head is only half of the procedure. You must also push the horse's hindquarters up underneath him so that he learns to travel in a frame. Teaching him first to give his head to bit pressure while on the ground helps the horse understand what you want when you use rein pressure. Pushing him into the bridle with your legs rounds the horse's back, making him travel in a frame. A horse cannot use himself properly, collect, or be physically prepared for the next maneuver if his hind end is strung out behind him. Rein pressure alone only tells a horse to stop and in no way helps him travel better. Use your legs to push the horse's hindquarters up underneath himself, making the horse use himself.

As soon as he gives to the bit—or drops his nose to a vertical position—and rounds his back, release the rein pressure to reward him and let him continue to move forward. You can verbally praise him the first few times to help him understand that he did the right thing. Then repeat. Gradually, ask him to hold it longer and longer.

Rather than looking to see if the horse's head is flexed at the poll, you only need to feel with your hands. If your hands stayed steady in the same place, as they should have, you'll no longer feel any pull or pressure on the reins. The horse will feel "soft" in your hands.

As you continue with this exercise, only ask the horse to give or flex for a few brief moments off and on throughout your schooling session. Over time, as he understands, gradually ask him to hold the flexed position for longer periods of time. Don't overdo it. Don't ask him to hold that position for long sessions, and don't ask him over and over again without rewarding him with a rest or a relaxing walk or trot on a long rein. Gradually asking him to extend the time that he holds the flexed position will let the horse understand, and it will allow his muscles to develop properly.

Gradually increase the amount of time your horse is in the flexed position. Be careful not to overdo this.

When you feel the horse soften in your hands, release the pressure to reward him. Reward the horse by releasing pressure every time that he gives to you. You "give" the horse back his "face" every time that he "gives" it to you. Slowly, over several weeks, you ask him to hold that position longer.

By teaching a horse to "give" to pressure, or to drop his nose to a vertical position, he learns through months of repetition that the proper response—the proper way to gain relief from pressure—is to flex at the poll and give his face.

Don't ask her to overflex. Sometimes going to a shank bit too quickly on a young horse will cause this to happen.

Teaching a horse to give to the bit, and keeping him trained to do so, requires that you have good hands and that you don't abuse the horse's mouth. The goal of any training procedure is to have a horse that responds to light, barely seen aids. Abusing a horse's mouth by pulling too hard, too often, or for unnecessary reasons will set your training back—possibly months. You must constantly be aware of what your hands are doing so that the horse will continue to improve.

A horse that flexes at the poll and gives to the bit, remaining soft and light in your hand, will not fight you. Almost always before a horse leaps sideways, tries to run through the bridle, or does any number of other evasive tactics, he will stick his nose in the air. If the horse keeps his head flexed, staying soft in the bridle, he is willing to listen and to do as you ask and will not run off.

SWITCHING TO A SHANK BIT

After training a horse to give to the bit through the use of a snaffle, as

After a period of training, he'll flex at the poll when he feels the slack come out of the rein.

mentioned earlier, you may ride him in a shank bit. A bit is only as strong as the hands that use it. I sometimes put a horse in a stronger bit so that he respects the signals given. I *don't* use a stronger bit so that I can pull harder— I use a stronger bit so that I can become *lighter*, or use less of a "pull." But, until a horse is trained to the signals of a bit, I stay with a snaffle or the lightest bit that the horse will respond to.

If you have a horse that does not listen with the bit you are using—and hopefully you have not abused his mouth by having heavy hands—try another bit. It does not always have to be stronger. Sometimes using just another type of bit will suffice. This exercise on bitting a horse must be done with some type of snaffle. While you are riding a horse, however, you may try different types of bits, keeping in mind that your safety is always the first concern.

When you start a horse, he may be unhappy in a certain type of bit. I start most of my horses in a hollow-mouth snaffle for a month or so, then move on to a thinner, sweet-iron snaffle. After training a horse in a snaffle, and putting a face on him, you may go on to a Mullen mouth bit, a low port, a straight bar, one with shanks that swivel or move independently from one another, or a solid, medium port bit. Find what bit your horse likes and the one in which he will perform the best.

See if your horse can carry the bit comfortably. Does he have a fat tongue? He may need a bit with a higher port, giving him some tongue relief. Does he chew or fuss with the bit at a standstill before you even get on his back? Has he been this way right from the start? Did you check for wolf teeth or sharp edges that may be causing him pain?

Every horse is different. Some horses are born with snaffle mouths and will listen in that type of bit forever. Other horses that are born that way are "toughened" by riders with heavy hands. A horse's mouth will become callused or the nerves will become deadened (just as your hands become callused and toughened by too much use). Find a bit that your horse works well in and one that he carries comfortably. As you continue to ride this horse, you may need to change the type of bit to get the desired response. Don't be afraid to change bits. Experiment. Just be sure that it is not *your* hands that are at fault. Remember that this cold piece of steel is in the horse's *mouth*.

If your horse won't listen in the bit that you are using, go to a somewhat stronger bit. Never sacrifice your safety. A horse must learn to obey the signals given by a bit. Going to a stronger bit, if you have good hands and don't abuse a horse's mouth, can actually make a horse become lighter.

CHAPTER SIX

Teaching Your Horse to Be Light

WHAT'S THE SECRET?

Have you ever seen a horse that responded to light, almost invisible aids? Do you wonder how you can train your horse to respond that way? The secret to teaching a horse to respond to a light aid is to apply the aids in the following sequence: First, *ask* him to obey a given cue; then give him a chance to obey. If he doesn't respond, *tell* him that he must obey the cue by using a slightly stronger aid. If he still doesn't respond, *enforce* the cue by using a stronger method. Your horse must learn that he must obey your cues when you ask him to obey. Yet, by asking in this sequence—*ask, tell, enforce*—you allow your horse the chance to respond to the light, asking aid to avoid the harsher telling or enforcing aid. Remember that the aids are *signals* to the horse—a way to ask him to respond, not a way to force him to respond. For example, a horse does not stop because you pull on the reins; he stops because you let go of the reins when he does stop. Therefore, you reward him for stopping.

You must be sure that your horse obeys an aid after you ask him, or he will learn that he does not have to obey *any*

of your aids. Yet, if you "tell" a horse to respond before you "ask" him, he will never have the opportunity to learn that he could have avoided the harsher cue simply by responding to the lighter one.

For a horse to learn, you must apply your aids consistently, in the same way, every time that you ask. You must expect to get results. Even a small step in the right direction is acceptable, because it means that the horse is trying

Splash backs on a light rein cue with diagonal pairs of legs moving backwards in cadence. At the top of the page, he lopes, stops, circles, and backs with only a light rope around his neck! It is the training, not the bit, that tells him to perform.

to understand what you are asking and he is trying to please you.

For example, when you initially start a colt under saddle, the colt has no way of knowing that a squeeze from your legs means to walk or jog or lope. He has had no prior experience to prepare him for this. Therefore, when you ride a colt for the first time, you must teach him the aids—that when you use your legs in a certain way, you are asking him to walk, jog, or lope.

To teach him to respond to the cue to walk, first squeeze lightly with both legs. If he does not walk, then bump him with both legs. As soon as he begins to walk, immediately stop bumping him to reward him for walking. After you have done this a few times, the colt

Roy Ferro, Joe's son, won the first large Open class at the first show put on by the NRHA on the old-type reining horse. A big bit was used to put the horse into the ground with no thought to the finesse we see today.

will walk when he feels the squeeze from your legs to avoid being bumped by your legs. You have shown him that it is more comfortable to walk from a squeeze than to get bumped. You have shown him that you will reward him— the bumping stops—for walking and obeying your aid. You have shown him that he can avoid the bumping by responding to your light "asking" aid— the squeeze.

If a colt does not walk from the "telling" aid—the bump—you would use a crop or bat and increase the severity of your leg cues to enforce the cue. The young horse thinks, "If she squeezes and I do not walk, she bumps me until I do walk. (Boy, is that uncomfortable and annoying!) Once I walk (as she asks), she stops bumping me and sits quietly. I think I'll try to walk the next time from the light squeeze so she won't bump me with her legs or tap my rump with the crop."

ASK, TELL, ENFORCE

This same sequence of ask, tell, and enforce is used on an older horse to teach him to respond to a light request. Make it uncomfortable for him to be wrong and comfortable for him to be right. Reward him for his good behavior by sitting quietly on his back. Once you ask for something, you are committed to getting it! For example, if your horse trots into the lope rather than going into a lope from a walk, you must correct him every time that he trots into the lope. Pull him back immediately to a walk. Then *immediately* ask him to lope again. Waiting longer than a few seconds to ask for the lope again will confuse him. He won't know why he is being corrected or how he can avoid it in the future. You must be clear about what your corrections mean.

Repeat the procedure if he trots again, pulling him back to a walk, but this time use a stronger "telling" aid to tell him to lope directly from the walk. If he trots into the lope again, make him walk again and use spurs to tell him to lope if you have a secure lower leg, or tap him with a crop. As soon as he begins to lope, release all cues and sit quietly. Reward him for loping from the walk. Be sure to *use your reins gently* when you do ask him to slow back to a walk so that he will not confuse just slowing down with your prior correction.

Use the same exact cues and the same exact sequence of cues for the same exact responses, every time. A horse will easily understand a cue and this sequence of ask, tell, enforce, if it is repeated consistently, enough times, *and if you use the same exact cue to mean the same exact thing, every time.* Horses learn through repetition. Talk to your horse in the same language so that he can understand what you are asking him to do. If I spoke to you in English on one day, Lithuanian on the second, and Chinese on the third, how much would you understand? Your horse often feels the same way. If every movement that you make on your horse's back means the same thing every time, imagine how quickly he will learn.

Yet, most people do not use their ability to ride so exactly and consistently. For example, if one time your horse departs correctly into a lope and you sit perfectly still, having given him the exact cue to lope at the exact time, you've rewarded him. The next time, however, your hand slips just as your horse lifts into the lope and you bump his mouth. Now he wonders, "Gee, did I do something wrong? Why did she bump me with the rein? Was that a correction?" Horses cannot understand, "I'm so sorry, my hand slipped. I didn't mean to bump your mouth." This same thing happens over and over again in

Joe's daughter, Joanne, carries on the tradition. Notice how soft the horse is in the bridle and that he paddles in front, rather than jamming or bracing his front legs in to the ground.

many different ways: You accidentally give slight corrections, and you assume that your horse should ignore them. Yet the more "accidents" that occur, the longer it takes for your horse to decipher which is a cue, which is a correction, and which is an accident.

Horses are creatures of habit. They like things to be neat, orderly, clear, and concise. Teach them exactly what you expect from them. Use each aid to mean the same thing every time that you apply it. Horses will learn to ignore aids if they are given indiscriminately or if they are not enforced. If you ask a horse to lope, make him lope. Make him obey your aids. He must first understand what you want; then he must obey to the best of his ability at that time.

Artificial aids can be used . . .

. . . to encourage your horse to go forward, but they must be used correctly.

If you use your aids at any time without enforcing them, you are actually teaching your horse to tune you out. If you ask him to walk, jog, or halt, yet when he does not respond, you continue to ask and ask and ask, yet never tell him or enforce the aid, he will learn to ignore you. If you ask a horse to obey, then change your mind and decide that the horse does not really have to obey, what have you just told him? That he can choose which aid he would like to obey? You *must* enforce your cues or else not ask him by applying a cue. Don't teach your horse that he does not have to obey your aids.

Ask him, tell him, then enforce your request. Make him respond. Give him

1. Ask
2. Tell
3. Enforce

the opportunity to obey the light aid in order to avoid the harsher telling aid.

NEVER JERK THE REINS

Besides using your leg aids to ask and then tell, you should also use your rein aids in the same manner. Never snatch at the reins (and therefore at a horse's mouth) when you want to tell him to slow or to halt. First, lightly pick up contact with his mouth. Only then should you lightly increase pressure or tension on the reins smoothly until the horse responds.

Never jerk on the reins unless you are applying an extreme correction, such as when a horse bucks. Even then, I choose to pull a horse in a few tight circles after I get his head up. Jerking on the reins can seriously damage the bars of a horse's mouth. It can cause a horse to become nervous and raise his head when he feels the least amount of bit pressure. Jerking or being too heavy on his mouth

can undo weeks of teaching him to give to the bit and flex at the poll. The horse will put his head in the air to save himself from the sharp pain that he associates with the bit when it is used incorrectly.

Remember that the bit or reins are the lines of communication to the horse. You cannot force a horse to stop—you can only apply an aid that tells him to stop. Jerking on the reins of a reining horse will usually cause him to get stiff throughout his entire body and jam his front legs into the ground when he is asked to stop. To teach a horse to respond to a light aid, you must teach him to trust that you will not hurt him when he has done nothing wrong. Don't abuse the trust a horse has in you.

There is a large difference between pulling and jerking. Picking up contact

> A horse does not stop because you pull on the reins; he stops because you let go when he does stop.

Pick up contact slowly.

Splash. Notice the soft cues and the big crossover step in front.

If every movement that you make on your horse's back means the same thing every time, imagine how quickly he will learn.

TALK SO THAT THE HORSE UNDERSTANDS

Think of the way a horse learns and then talk to your horse in a language that he can understand. Teach him what you expect from each cue, and then give him the opportunity to respond to a light, asking aid before you tell him. This sequence of ask and then tell can be applied to almost every part of training.

The only time that I do not ask first is when a horse is misbehaving. If a horse tries to buck, do not ask him nicely to stop bucking—*tell him!* Bucking is unacceptable at any time. Give him a strong correction—instantly. Leave no doubt in his mind that he was wrong and that he will be punished immediately. Kicking at another horse or trying to bite are also unacceptable. But for the horse that is going along, doing what he should be doing, give him the opportunity to respond to a light aid by asking first and then telling. Let him avoid a harsher aid. Reward him for doing as you have asked by sitting quietly on his back and leaving him alone.

In time, you should see an improvement in your horse's responsiveness. Think of each small step you gain as another step up the ladder to becoming a better rider—a quiet, soft-talking, "thinking" rider.

and slowly increasing the pressure is acceptable—jerking is not. If you find that your horse will not stop, go back to the round pen, put a chain under his nose, and teach him the meaning of the word "Whoa!"

CHAPTER SEVEN

Teaching Your Horse to Follow His Nose

A TRAINING BASIC

Whether your horse is headed for a career as a reiner, a Western pleasure horse, or a trail horse, he must be taught to "follow his nose." The basis of all training is for a horse to go forward on command and to follow his nose. When he has learned this you can control the direction in which he travels. In order for a horse to circle correctly, whether it is a circle in a reining pattern or a circle in a horsemanship class, he must bend his head, neck and rib cage into the correct arc of the circle. If a horse tries to keep his body in a straight line while circling, the circle will look and feel more like an octagon. He will throw his hip to the outside of the circle rather than bending or arcing his body correctly. If his head and neck remain straight and he leans into a turn while circling, like a motorcycle cornering at high speeds, he will not stay upright and balanced. If he is not upright and balanced, he will be unable to perform the next maneuver that you ask of him.

The horse must bend his head and neck and his middle or rib cage into the correct arc of the circle. I often exaggerate a cue in the beginning and then lighten up later.

Adjust the nose band so two fingers will fit between the nose band and your horse's nose.

On this young Hollywood Dun It filly who is just beginning her career, boots protect her front legs from bumps and bruises, a cavesson reminds her to keep her mouth closed, and the snaffle bit and running martingale help teach head position.

BEGIN TRAINING WITH A SNAFFLE

When you are ready to start this training, put a saddle and a bridle with a snaffle bit—one without shanks—on your horse. Adding a chin strap to the snaffle will help so that the bit cannot be pulled through the horse's mouth. Some horses will open their mouth to evade the pressure from the bit, and the rings of the bit can be pulled right through their mouth.

USING A CAVESSON

If you see your horse opening his mouth throughout this training, add a cavesson or noseband. A dropped noseband will help to teach a horse that he must not open his mouth. Adjust the cavesson somewhat snugly; you should be able to insert just two fingers between the horse and the noseband. Give the horse a few minutes to adjust to the feel of the noseband, then take hold of the reins and lightly guide the horse's head first left, then right. Next, take both reins and ask the horse to back up. Let him know that you have added new equipment and that he can no longer open his mouth quite so readily. He may react to a cavesson by tossing his head or fighting the bit when you tie his head side to side. The cavesson will teach him that opening his mouth is not acceptable, but watch him the first time or two. It is better to be prepared and give the horse time to accept this restraint before getting into a fight. Don't just expect your horse to take it in stride.

TYING THE REINS

Tie the off-side rein loosely to the saddle horn. It must be loose enough so that the horse can comfortably turn his head in the opposite direction (the direction in which you tie him) without him feeling restricted in any way. For this exercise, the horse should only have to contend with the feeling of the rein on one side. Tie the rein on the side to which you want the horse to bend to the back ring of your saddle or the top section of the girth. First, let the horse's head and neck extend straight forward. Then gradually tighten the rein to get a slight bend in the horse's neck. Tie the rein at that point with a quick-release knot (for safety reasons). If your horse gets into trouble, you only need to pull the end of the rein and his head will be untied. However, do not be in a hurry to untie the horse if he only fusses a little. He must learn that fighting will get him nowhere.

Always tie the horse loosely with just a *slight* bend for the first few days.

Anytime you tie a horse's head, use a snaffle bit.

This slight bend gives the horse less reason to fight. The pressure on the rein will only come into play if he tries to put his head and neck straight forward. Tying him loosely the first few days will teach him that he must obey the pressure on the rein, no matter how slight, to gain relief from pressure on his mouth. He will learn to "give" or to bend his head in response to the rein pressure. After a few days you can tie the rein a bit tighter and you will see the horse beginning to drop his head and flex at the poll.

This exercise in tying a horse's head accomplishes two things. He learns to follow the bend of his neck and thus follows his nose when you ask him to walk forward. As you progress and increase the tension on the rein, he will find that it is easier to make a circle and follow his nose around that circle. If you let him stand tied this way, he also learns to drop his head and flex at the poll as another way of gaining relief from pressure.

Start with five minutes on each side the first day and work your way up to fifteen to twenty minutes on each side. If your horse is very quiet, you may need to swish a longe whip on the ground to ask him to follow his nose and circle. Only use as much whip pressure as needed to make the horse walk. Don't get him excited and racing around these little circles since that defeats the purpose of this soft, quiet training.

It may be necessary for you to vary your position to keep the horse moving. As with longeing, you must stay behind the horse. Getting in front of the line where your stirrup would hang will block a horse's forward movement. If you find that your horse is stiffer on one

Tie the outside rein loosely to the saddle horn.

Tie the rein in the direction that you wish the horse to bend in, to the back ring of the saddle or to the girth.

side than the other, increase the amount of time that he is tied on the stiff side. If your horse ever decides that he will not turn in one direction, barring a physical reason, you can dismount and tie his head on the offending side and let him stand for twenty minutes.

You can tie your horse before you ride him, or you can tie him and ride him later. When you do begin to ride, ask your horse to make a series of large circles. Gain contact with your direct rein to ask your horse to turn, and apply your neck-rein cue as well. Put your inside leg at the girth to ask the horse to move his rib cage in an arc to the outside. Use your outside leg to hold the horse's hip in the direction of the arc. Don't let him swing his rump to the outside of the circle. His body should be in the correct shape of an arc that conforms to the size of the circle. If you ever feel the horse falling into the circle or dropping his in-

> **When you ask a horse to bend, you should see just the corner of his eye on a large circle, more on a smaller circle.**

side shoulder, lift your inside rein to lift his shoulder. Lifting a horse's shoulder is discussed in more detail in Chapter 9. Lifting your inside rein will lift the horse's inside shoulder and make him more upright and balanced. Remember—this is training, not equitation. Your pulling hand may end up twelve inches above the saddle horn. That is perfectly acceptable at this stage.

When you ask a horse to bend, watch the position of his head and neck. You should just see the corner of his eye on a large circle—more on a smaller circle. Try to feel whether he is bending nicely, arcing correctly around the circle, or if he is throwing his hip to the outside or dropping a shoulder. If he is not obeying your direct-rein cue, you will feel the resistance in your direct rein. He should follow the bend, and the rein will feel soft in your hands. If he tugs to the outside on every other step, you will know that he has not yet learned to give. More tying from the ground will help to alleviate this problem. Keep on training. In a couple of weeks you should begin to see an improvement.

CORRECTING PROBLEMS

If your horse does not bend, or will not circle, first gain contact with the inside rein and then "pull" him around the circle. If he fights, lock your hand on your hip and hold it there so that the horse cannot pull the rein out of your hand. Force him to bend. His head and neck may become overbent as you do this, but after a time or two, he should give in. Then you can lighten up the pressure and ask him to bend around a circle on a lighter rein.

Also, feel if the horse is throwing his hip to the outside of the circle. If he is, make your circles a bit larger so that he can comfortably learn to follow his nose. Apply your outside leg behind the girth to hold his hip in the correct arc of the circle.

A horse must learn in stages. First, you teach him to obey leg and rein pressure, and later those same aids are used to add finesse to each maneuver. Training must be broken down into small segments for a horse to learn.

Ask your horse to bend in two or three medium-small circles. If the horse resists or fights, force him to bend and to follow his nose for another two or three circles. Then let him walk forward and ask again. If you get two nice circles, let your horse walk forward to reward him. Walk or jog around the arena for a few minutes and ask for a circle again. Because you are asking the horse to use new muscles, do not overdo this training in the initial stages. If he gets sore too often, he may become resentful and may fight you rather than give in and learn.

If your horse will not bend with his body in a correct arc—one that conforms to the size of the circle that you

Ask your horse to circle right with a right direct rein and your (right) leg at the girth. Always look where you are going!

This stallion lopes a circle and correctly stays upright and balanced. He is not leaning into the circle as he would if he dropped his inside shoulder (which would be incorrect). This is your goal, what your horse should look like when he circles.

If he fights, lock your hand on your hip and force him to turn—don't let him win this fight and pull the rein from your hand. However, if it happens often, check for a physical problem such as wolf teeth or teeth that need to be floated. Be sure to loosen the outside rein so he has freedom of his head to turn to the inside.

chose—continue to ask him to bend until you get one step correctly. Reward him for that one step, then ask him again and try to get two steps. Reward him for two steps by letting him walk straight forward for ten feet and ask again, this time looking for three steps.

BEGIN SLOWLY

Begin your initial training at a walk and increase to a jog only after your horse shows you that he understands. Adding speed increases the difficulty of any maneuver, and it is best to accomplish a new maneuver at the slower speeds before increasing the gait. You may have to spend two days or two weeks walking sets of two to three circles and then releasing to let the horse walk on a straight line.

This is hard work for your horse, so don't expect him to walk in tiny circles for half an hour at a time. Vary the routine. Slow time spent now on these ba-

sics will help you later. Any time that you lose now will be made up later. Never rush a horse or expect him to learn overnight. Take things easy and slow and show your horse what you want. Always reward him so that he understands he performed as you requested.

JOGGING IN CIRCLES

When you progress to jogging, the circles should be a bit larger to compensate for this increase in speed. You still want the horse to carry his body in the correct arc of the circle. To vary the routine, you can serpentine back and forth across the arena, perhaps making a full circle if it seems like the horse does not want to bend in exactly the right way. Changing the routine will keep your horse listening and waiting for your cues. Any time your horse tries to outguess you by choosing the direction in which to travel, it is a good time to "change his mind" and change direc-

Jog down the rail.

Make a small circle off the rail.

tions. Doing so will help to keep your horse obedient to your cues. For example, if he wants to make a turn to the left, change directions and ask him to go to the right. Another exercise is to follow the rail for ten to twenty feet, then make a medium-sized circle to the inside. When you meet the rail again, follow the rail for twenty feet and again make a circle to the inside. Continue this exercise all the way around the arena.

LOPING IN CIRCLES

Once your horse guides well and is obedient to your cues, begin to lope in circles using the method described above. Lope along the rail. Then lope in a circle to the inside, come back to the rail, and lope for ten or fifteen feet before making another circle. Be sure

that your horse stays upright and doesn't fall into the circle or drop his shoulder to the inside. Lope in circles in the center of the arena, bring him back to a jog, and then lope in the opposite direction.

Eventually, you should begin to see an improvement in how your horse bends and guides. There is no quick and easy fix—just hours in the saddle, always praising your horse for behaving to the best of his ability by sitting quietly, and correcting him when he is wrong. Given time, your horse will learn to follow his nose with either the direct rein or the neck rein. When you progress to teaching him to move from leg pressure, you can use your legs to increase or decrease the size of your circles.

> Changing the exercise routine will keep your horse listening and waiting for your cues.

Make him follow his nose as you come off the rail and circle.

CHAPTER EIGHT

Moving From Leg Pressure

LEG PRESSURE MEANS MORE THAN "GO"

Your horse is not truly broke until you can put his body in whatever position you want it to be. That includes using your legs to move him over, move him sideways, and move him forward. Teaching your horse to move away from leg pressure will enable you to teach him to spin, to roll back, to fix your circles, and to move laterally in either direction. If up to this point your horse only thinks of leg pressure as meaning "go," these exercises will help him learn that leg pressure can also mean to move his hip to enforce a straight-line backup, to move sideways during a spin, or to correct a drifting hip as he circles.

I start this leg-pressure training as soon as a horse understands to walk, jog, and lope, and also to turn his head in response to rein pressure. First, I tie a horse's from head side to side, as discussed in the chapter on bitting, so that he understands that when I take hold of one rein to bend his head, he should "give" to the rein pressure. As he progresses through this training, I want the horse to bend his head to the right in response to a right direct rein. Eventually, when I apply right leg pressure at the girth, he'll learn to arc his body in the shape of a "C" and move laterally to the left.

Tying a horse side to side teaches him to hit the bit and then back off from the pressure to reward himself. The horse learns to give to the rein pressure to reward himself. Tying a horse also helps to teach him to lighten up and obey your rein cues more readily.

If your horse seems stiffer or more resentful on one side, first check for a physical problem. Barring that, tie your horse a bit longer on the stiff side so that he can stretch those muscles. This will also help him learn that he must obey a command given on either side. However, do not neglect his good side. Otherwise, very soon his good side will become his bad side, and vice versa.

WARM UP FIRST

After you tie your horse from side to side, mount up and warm him up first. Walk him in large, bending circles or serpentines, stretching both sides of his body. Then jog, again working both sides to stretch his muscles. Lope for a few

Lift your arm up to keep the horse's shoulder elevated.

Lift your hand up to ask to bend. Soon he'll learn to bend and flex at the poll from this cue.

minutes. When he is settled and ready to go to work, ask him to walk in a small circle. Depending on the size of your horse, the circle may be from ten to fifteen feet across. He should be able to walk comfortably around this circle without crossing over with his front legs, but the circle should not be so large that the horse's body does not bend.

Keep your outside rein loose so that the horse can freely turn his head into the circle. Place the rein over his neck as you would for a neck-rein cue, but do not pull so hard that it tips his head in the opposite direction. Pick up contact with your inside rein. Raise that hand slightly to lift his inside shoulder. Gently guide him in the direction of your circle, and then release. Continue to pick up contact, bend the horse around the circle, and release.

A horse is not truly broke until you can put his body in whatever position you want it to be.

Keeping your elbow locked at your side and only using your forearm to lift and turn the horse will help insure that you are asking the horse correctly. Using your entire arm to lift the horse may cause you to use too much rein pressure. Try to use the least amount of pressure possible to keep him bending in a small, walking circle. You want the horse to think and to respond to the lightest of cues. Don't do the horse's work for him by pulling him around the entire circle. Make him think about and pay attention to your cues.

USE YOUR LEG

As your horse is walking and bending around this small circle, start teaching him to move away from leg pressure by putting your inside leg slightly behind the girth and pushing your heel into his side. When he responds

Throwing his hip to the outside is acceptable for this exercise.

See him step to the outside with his hind legs as you apply inside (left) leg pressure.

correctly, you will feel his hip move to the outside of your circle as his inside hind leg crosses over his outside hind leg. Exaggerate the cue initially and push your heel into his side. If he is very responsive or touchy, lighten up the cue. Use enough pressure so that your horse can feel it and understand that this is a new cue. Your horse should just be able to walk this circle comfortably.

Done correctly, you will feel the horse throwing his hip to the outside of this small circle when you apply heel pressure behind the girth. You may not get him to move his hip to the outside on every step, but strive for at least a step or two in each small circle. Throwing his hip to the outside is acceptable in this exercise. By teaching the horse to move away from leg pressure now, you can use your outside leg later to correct the horse from throwing his hip to the outside.

Walk two or three small circles. Try to feel the horse's hip move to the outside for a step or two in each circle. Then let the horse walk forward out of the cir-

cle. This is his reward for performing correctly. Be sure he is responding correctly to your aids before you "open the door" and let him walk out of the circle. If the horse is tossing his head or is fighting you in any way, keep asking him to bend and walk this small circle. Only when he gives in and performs correctly should you let him walk out of the circle.

As you progress through this logical succession of cues, your horse will begin to learn to move his hip in response to leg pressure. The smallness of the circle will keep him slow if he at first tries to rush in response to your heel pressure. He is learning that leg pressure can mean to move sideways as well as to move forward or faster.

ACHIEVE FORWARD MOTION

Forward motion is important. If the horse is lagging, bump him with your *outside* leg. Let him know that this is work and that you expect him to pay attention to you and respond correctly. Don't let him lug on the bit or pull or drop his inside shoulder and fall into the circle. A few bumps from your outside leg or lifting your inside rein hand to lift his shoulder should put his attention back on you, where it belongs.

Don't confuse a horse by switching from the left side to the right side and back again. Make your circles on the left side, walk forward twenty feet, and then repeat more circles on the left side. Do three sets of circles on one side before changing to the other side. If you're satisfied with the way your horse has responded, change sides and do three more sets of three circles. Then go on and work other maneuvers. If the horse needs more time on one side than the other, go back and work on the problem side. Six sets of three circles each set are enough for one lesson. Horses seem to learn if left overnight to think about a new maneuver. The following day, you may notice that your horse has taken a jump forward from his schooling of the previous day.

How Many Circles?

The number of walking circles depends on the horse. If he is doing well and showing no signs of resistance, two or three circles are enough. If the horse fights or shows signs of resentment, do five or six circles—even ten. However, if your horse is really fighting you, look for a physical reason. Check for wolf teeth if he tosses his head or tries to evade the bit, or look at his legs and hooves to see if he feels sore. If you do not find a physical cause, try to think back and see if you have confused him. Go back over his training and do something that the horse knows until you can figure out what has happened. Occasionally, a horse will just be having a bad day. Simply waiting until the next day may fix the problem with no other treatment. On the other hand, the horse

may be testing you. You may need to hold your hand on your hip and fight it out with him. Sometimes, a horse needs to understand that he must obey your cues.

TEACH THE SIDEPASS

After two to four weeks of asking your horse to move his hip to the outside of these small circles, begin to teach him to move his entire body away from leg pressure. Your timing of when to move on will depend on how often you ride and on how your horse has accepted the training to date. Let the horse tell you when to advance and when to retreat by his actions or response. You always want to have a solid base of training before you continue.

Begin by asking your horse to make three sets of circles on each side and then

Let the horse tell you when to advance your lessons.

walk straight across the arena. With a rein in each hand, pick up light contact with both reins so that if the horse tries to jog in response to leg pressure, you can gently ask him to walk again. Take a light hold of your left rein, and put your left leg into the horse's side at the girth. If you were to put your leg behind the girth, as you did to tell the horse to move his hip, he would be correct in moving only his hip. Now you want to ask the horse to move his entire body to the left in response to leg pressure, so you will put your leg at the girth.

Lift your inside rein and use inside leg pressure at the girth.

Your horse should take a step to the outside, closer to the rail.

Help the horse understand this new cue to move his entire body by picking up his left shoulder with your left rein and holding that rein straight above his mane. Do not cross his neck. Use your right rein to lightly direct rein him to the right if needed for the first few steps, or until he understands. Hold even pressure against his neck with the left rein; this will create a small bend to the left as you push your left leg at the girth. In the beginning, one small sideways step is perfectly acceptable. When you feel an attempt, release all pressure and let the horse walk straight forward. Praise him for doing well. Your timing in the release of all aids is extremely important and is what tells the horse that he did as you asked. Be willing to accept small segments of progress at first as you teach the horse this new cue.

You can also help your horse understand this new cue by putting weight on your right hip. Exaggerate at first. Put most of the weight from your seat on the right side of the saddle. The horse will move to the right, not only in response to your left-leg cue, but because your seat will feel off balance to

If you put weight to the right side of the saddle, your horse will step to the right to rebalance. Reward him for that one step. (Notice that my leg is now off his side.)

Releasing all cues is the reward when your horse does as you ask.

him. Stepping to the right puts your weight back in the center of the saddle where it belongs. If your horse moves even one small step, relax your aids, praise your horse, and go back to your normal position in the saddle. This rewards the horse and tells him that he did as you asked.

If your horse tries to increase his speed in response to your leg pressure (a natural response in the initial stages of training), do not punish him. Instead, bring him gently back to a walk. The next time that you cue him, be prepared with your reins to keep him at a walk. Increase the tension on the reins just enough that he can feel the pressure. Only increase your rein pressure if your horse starts to move forward faster than a walk when you ask him to move laterally or sideways with your leg. Now ask again. If you get one step, relax your aids and praise him.

WATCH YOUR TIMING

Timing is crucial in any aspect of training, as is the repetition of cues so that the cues become a habit for your horse to perform. Releasing all cues when he does as you ask is a big reward to a horse. In addition, you may use a verbal "Good boy" and scratch or rub his neck to praise him, but releasing your aids is the most important.

Asking for one step, three or four times the first day, is enough. Make that be the last thing for which you ask. In this way, when the horse responds correctly and gives you that one step, you can stop him, sit on his back for a moment praising him, and then dismount right there. Put him away and let him think about what caused him to get such a big reward. This leaves the new exercise fresh in the horse's mind and

lets him think about it overnight. When you bring the horse out the next day, he should give you that one step quite readily. Patience is essential. Continue to ask for just one step on the following three or four days. As the horse progresses and gives you one step readily, then you can ask for two steps and then three steps.

After the first couple of days, you should no longer have to weight one side of your saddle. You should only use that additional cue the first day or two to help your horse understand. Now he should move from a leg cue alone. Don't overdo this exercise; it is hard work for your horse and uses a new group of muscles. You can undo your training by asking a horse for too much, too soon, making him become sore and resentful.

TEACH THE COUNTERBEND

Once a horse reaches the stage where he will move three or four steps in response to leg pressure, you can begin to teach him to counterbend. For this exercise, you will ask him to arc his body in the opposite direction from that in which you want him to move. For example, tip his head to the right by using a right direct rein so that you can see the corner of his right eye. Now push him to the left with your right leg. He should be bent around your right leg with his spine bent in the shape of a "C," looking to the right, yet he will move diagonally forward to the left in response to your right leg at the girth (see the photos for a visual example). Accomplishing this at a jog is sometimes easier than at a walk, although in time he should perform the maneuver at a walk, jog, and lope. It may take from two to four months to teach a horse to be really responsive to

Counterbend to the right. Left rein, left leg.

Counterbend to the left. Right rein, right leg. Notice my left leg is off her side to "open the door" and give her a place to go that is not blocked by pressure.

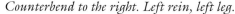

your legs and perform the counterbend at all gaits.

I teach this exercise to every horse that I train, whether they are headed for a life as a reiner, a hunter, a Western pleasure horse, or a trail horse. A reining horse must learn this cue before you can teach him to spin or to roll back, and to correct his circles if he begins to drift. If your trail horse is not approaching the center point of an obstacle, you can use your leg to move his entire body toward the center of the obstacle. On occasion, you may need to push a horse's hip in one direction or the other so that his approach to an ob-

stacle is straight. In a rail class, rather than overtly reining your horse in or out away from the rail, you can use leg-pressure cues to ask him to move over. It will make you look more polished than if you steer your horse in big, sweeping turns in and out away from the rail.

As you gain control of your horse's hip and shoulders, you will be able to put your horse in almost any position that you choose. Remember that it takes time for a horse to understand these new cues. Don't rush your horse through this training. The result will be a movable, supple, well-trained horse.

Queenie counterbending nicely on soft cues. Don't use more force than is necessary.

CHAPTER NINE

Lifting a Shoulder

USES FOR THE LIFT

Teaching your horse a specific cue to lift his shoulders will later allow you to use that same cue to teach him to spin and to roll back correctly. A reining horse must elevate both shoulders in order to turn around in a spin. He must move the inside front shoulder back and out of the way, allowing his outside front leg to move *in front of* his inside leg. This, combined with the inside hind-pivot leg remaining locked in place, creates the spin. The same is true of the rollback. The horse must elevate his shoulders to lift them up and over his hocks in order to turn and head back in the opposite direction.

You can also use this cue to correct a horse if he tries to drop a shoulder and fall into his circles, or if he tries to run out of a circle. In order to stop and "get into the ground," a horse must elevate his shoulders and drop his hindquarters closer to the ground. When a horse does not change leads correctly, or misses or drags a lead behind, the cause is often a dropped shoulder. The cue itself is simple, yet *feeling* a dropped shoulder may not be so easy initially, at least for the novice rider.

RECOGNIZING A DROPPED SHOULDER

If your horse feels like he is falling to the inside of his circles, the cause is most likely a dropped inside shoulder. To lope in a correct circle, your horse must stay upright and balanced. He should not feel like a motorcycle cornering at high speeds, laying down into the corners.

If your horse tries to drift to the outside of a circle, it is probably caused by a dropped outside shoulder. If your horse's head is bent into the circle, yet he drifts to the outside, dropping his outside shoulder allows him to sneak to the outside of the circle. Rather than lifting your inside rein, as you might think would be the correct response (to guide him back into the circle), you must lift the *outside* rein. This will lift your horse's outside shoulder and force him to stay upright.

CUEING THE HORSE TO LIFT HIS SHOULDER

To teach a horse the cue for lifting his shoulder, first walk him along a wall or a fence, three to four feet to the inside.

Walk your horse along the fence with the fence on your left.

Lift your left inside rein . . .

. . . to lift your horse's shoulder and make the turn.

When the horse is settled and paying attention to you, turn him into the fence using the following sequence of cues:

1. Lift the rein closest to the fence about four to six inches higher than normal, keeping contact with the bit. This lifts the horse's shoulder.

2. As you lift or hold his shoulder up, also turn the horse in toward the fence by bringing your inside raised hand out somewhat (to create the turn toward the fence) just long enough to make the horse turn into the fence.

3. Ask the horse to *move away from leg pressure* as you would in a roll back. Push the horse with your outside leg, using enough pressure so that the horse can feel your leg. A quiet or dead-sided horse needs more pressure than a light or responsive horse.

4. When the horse is committed to the turn, leaving him no choice but to turn or risk hitting his nose on the fence (should he choose to go back in the same direction), bring your hand back to an upright, raised position and let the fence turn the horse.

5. *You should feel the horse's inside shoulder lift up and move back out of the way (making room for his outside leg to cross over and make the turn).*

Simultaneously release your rein cues and let the horse finish the turn on his own. If the horse slows or stops, use your outside leg to bump him and send him forward down the fence.

This series of cues combined with the proximity to the fence forces the horse naturally to lift his inside shoulder up and move it back out of the way. It allows his outside front leg room to go over and across his inside front leg and make the turn. (This is the same movement that he will need later when learning to spin.) If your horse does this correctly, or at least attempts to, let him walk forward down the fence on a loose rein with your body relaxed to tell him that you are pleased with the way he responded. This is his reward and tells him that he was correct.

PROBLEMS?

If the horse did not lift his shoulder, move him closer to the fence and ask again. Being closer to the fence *naturally* forces the horse to lift his inside shoulder and back it out of the way to allow room to maneuver the other front leg around and make the turn. Again, if he does it correctly, release your aids and let the horse walk forward to tell him that you are pleased.

Some horses need to be very close to the fence, at least in the initial stages of training, to force them to lift their inside shoulder up and back out of the way. Others will understand easily at a farther distance. As with anything concerning horses, there is no set rule. You must experiment to find what works best when teaching any new training maneuver or cue to each horse.

If the horse loses the impulsion or energy necessary to complete the turn, use your outside leg to bump him forward. This exercise should be done at

Dropping your hand below the saddle horn can cause a horse to drop his shoulder.

Lift your hand up to keep her shoulder up.

a walk, so only use as much energy as needed to keep the horse walking. Teaching this exercise at a walk helps the horse remain calm and learn the cue without becoming excited or nervous.

As your horse gains in understanding, a soft, light cue creates a soft, light response. Both horses are still in a snaffle. It doesn't take a strong bit; it takes light hands.

Get Help From a Ground Person

If you cannot feel the lift of the inside shoulder, ask a friend or a ground person to watch the horse's inside shoulder. He will actually see the horse's inside shoulder blade move up and back out of the way when done correctly. If an assistant can tell you when the horse is lifting his inside shoulder, you will learn to feel the moment. Be sure to release the rein pressure to reward the horse when he lifts that shoulder.

Adding speed always increases the degree of difficulty.

Practice This at the End of a Lesson

In the initial stages of training, I ask the horse to perform this exercise at the end of the lesson, when I am walking him to cool him down. He should be somewhat tired and ready to listen. Walk down the fence, elevate his inside shoulder, turn, release, and walk on. Reverse your cues and repeat in the opposite direction. Do this five or six times per side if the horse is responding correctly. Then dismount and put him away to leave the new cue fresh in his mind and reward him for doing as you asked.

Repeat the Steps

Repeating these steps daily will teach your horse that when you lift your rein, he must lift the corresponding shoulder. He should show little or no sign of resistance to this new cue when you later use it at the jog or lope. Using the fence does a large part of the work for you and allows you to teach this exercise quietly and calmly. When you begin to use this cue at a lope, such as when your horse drops a shoulder while circling, the horse should understand the cue from the prior fence training. He should not throw his head to evade the cue.

Adding speed always increases the degree of difficulty. Continue working on this exercise at a walk, using the fence for as many days as it takes for both you and your horse to understand.

Dropping his left inside shoulder. See how he is "falling to the inside"?

Pick the inside rein up to lift his inside shoulder.

Wait until you can feel the horse lift his shoulder in response to your rein cue before you move on. Work both sides equally, or work a little longer on the stiffer side.

USING THE CUE

When both you and your horse understand the concept of lifting a shoulder, you can begin to use it in your daily work. If you are making a circle and the horse starts floating to the inside of the circle because he has dropped his inside shoulder, lift your inside rein to lift the horse's inside shoulder. Gain contact with the horse's mouth, lift him up to tell him to travel upright and balanced, send him on, and then release. You should feel the horse lift up and feel as if he is now "upright and between the bridle." "Between the bridle" means that the horse is moving in an upright position, staying balanced, dropping neither his left nor his right shoulder, nor leaning to the left or to the right. If his left shoulder is dropped, you will feel as if you are leaning to the left, because

And then release to reward him. You must teach him to travel upright and balanced!

that shoulder is closer to the ground than the right shoulder. Both shoulders of your horse should be upright and balanced. A horse that is upright and between the bridle has no choice but to move straight forward.

Your horse can also drop an outside shoulder, which may be a bit more

You may need to pop the rein upward once or twice to get his attention, especially on an older horse that tries to ignore you.

difficult for you to feel, at least in the initial stages. It is not quite as obvious as dropping an inside shoulder. If your horse is bending his head in the correct direction of your circle, yet drifting to the *outside* of the circle, lift your *outside* rein to correct him. The horse will now become upright and balanced and will move straight forward along the path of the circle.

Any time you are loping circles and feel your horse drop a shoulder, pick up the corresponding rein to correct the dropped shoulder. Then release the rein pressure and continue. If the horse drops a shoulder again, just pick up a rein to correct, release, and go on. Don't make it a big deal—just correct him and go on. If he really tries to evade your cues, perhaps to run out near a gate, you can pop the rein upward a time or two to put his attention back on his work, but usually, lifting the rein will suffice. When training horses, I often ride with two hands so that it is easier to fix a problem such as this.

RIDE STRAIGHT LINES

If you ride continuously in a round pen, or in small circles, you may actually teach your horse to drop his shoulders. You must also get the horse out and ride him in straight lines. A good exercise is to ride square circles. A square or rectangular pen becomes four straight lines with four quarter-turns. When you ask the horse to turn the quarter-circle, raise your inside hand to remind him to lift that inside shoulder and stay upright as he makes the turn. If he does not pay attention to your lifted hand, pop the rein upward once or twice to make him respect your cue. While it is not a good practice to jerk on a horse's mouth, this is one situation where a horse may benefit from a little upward "pop" of the reins. Used once or twice, it should cause your horse to pay attention and be obedient to your cues. If it continues to be a problem, you may need to look further back in your horse's training or work longer on the serpentine exercise. A well-trained horse should be able to ride in a straight line or circle on command.

Riding square circles gives you the added benefit of staying off the horse's mouth during the straight-line segment of the circle. If you are constantly applying pressure to your horse, he will, in time, learn to tune you out. Every training procedure with a horse requires give and take. You *take* the rein and lift him up, then *give* him back his face to reward him. In this way, your cues become lighter and lighter. Your horse learns that there is a reward for doing as you ask. He will try to achieve that reward (a loose rein) by responding more quickly to the correction (the raised rein).

USING THE CUE TO CHANGE LEADS

Another area where this cue comes in handy is on lead changes. A horse cannot change leads if his shoulder is dropped or his weight is all on his forehand. For a horse to change leads cleanly, or correctly—both front and back—he must reach under himself with his hind leg to *initiate* the change of leads. In this way, he can change leads from back to front. An old method of changing leads was to ask for the change of leads while loping over a log on the ground. The reason this was effective was because the horse had to elevate his shoulders to get over the log. Once he elevated his shoulders, it was easy for the horse to reach underneath and change leads with a hind leg first. He is in the air for that split second longer, allowing him to change leads behind first.

A well-trained horse should be able to ride in a straight line or circle on command.

OTHER USES FOR THE CUE TO LIFT A SHOULDER

As you progress with your horse's training, you will need this simple cue to teach your horse to roll back, to spin, and to help with sliding stops. If your horse begins to miss or drag a lead behind, this simple cue may be your answer. If he drops a shoulder and runs out of your circles, you can use this cue to lift his shoulder and send him straight forward. Teaching this cue is another step in the training program and another way to have more control over your horse. While it may be confusing to feel at first, once you ride and understand the feeling of a dropped shoulder, it should become second nature to fix it.

CHAPTER TEN

Using the Serpentine to Add Precision

TRAINING WITH THE SERPENTINE

Using this serpentine exercise will teach your horse to go straight and to follow his nose. It will also help your horse to bend correctly and to keep him from relying on a fence line or rail. A rider who uses both hand and leg aids now will help the young horse to associate the proper cues with the proper response later. By teaching a horse to follow his nose on a straight path and to bend correctly around the half-circle, you are laying a good foundation for later work, no matter what discipline you choose.

School your horse in a snaffle bit if possible for this serpentine exercise. This will allow you to use a direct-rein pull as needed.

The only other requirement for this exercise is a large, flat space in which to ride—either an arena or a flat pasture. Be sure that your horse is properly warmed up before beginning this exercise. Bends and transitions are hard work for a horse. Give him time to loosen up physically and to be mentally prepared to pay attention to what you are asking of him.

While working at the slower gaits, such as a walk or a jog, use the width of your arena and serpentine that way. When you progress to the extended trot or the lope, use the longer length of your arena so that your horse has room to move out.

USE A VISUAL AID

To begin, pick a visual point directly across from where you plan to start. You can choose either a tree or a fence post or any other visual aid to give you a direct-line reference point toward which to ride. Split your reins and hold one in each hand. With the horse "held between your hands," ask him to walk in a straight line toward your chosen marker. If your horse deviates from this path, use your hand and leg aids to tell him that you want him to walk straight toward your chosen visual point.

Find a visual reference and ride toward it in a straight line.

Pick a visual point and look up.

Traci chose the tree as her visual aid and rode straight toward it.

TEACH YOUR HORSE TO STAY UPRIGHT

If your horse drops his right shoulder and begins to duck out to the right, use the right rein to lift or elevate his right shoulder. This will cause him to stay upright and between the bridle. If he is balanced, with neither shoulder dropped, he should walk straight forward. Be sure to sit quietly and release all cues when the horse is walking straight forward. This tells him that he is responding correctly. Repeat the correction as needed by lifting your rein on the side on which his shoulder drops. When he is correct, sit quietly. If you feel his hindquarters drift to one side or the other, use the corresponding leg to push his hip back in line.

If your horse tries to duck out or to turn to the left to avoid working, direct rein him to the right—*the opposite direction from what he chooses*. Turn him in two to three tight circles as a correction, then let him walk forward again. If he tries to duck out to the right, circle him to the left. Once you have made two or three correction circles, release your aids to allow the horse to continue on the straight-line path that he was following before you corrected him. Notice at what point you must release your aids to make your horse follow a straight line toward your visual aid. This knowledge of how your horse responds to a given cue may come in handy later. Notice, too, how little or much pressure it takes for your horse to return correctly to the straight line.

If you drop your hand, it will cause your horse to drop his (left) inside shoulder.

You must keep your hand up . . .

Your horse should be walking energetically, not just poking along. If he will not walk in an energetic, four-beat rhythm, ask him to increase his pace by alternately squeezing and releasing his sides slightly faster than his current walking rhythm. If he ignores your asking command, tell him to move forward with more energy by alternately bumping him with one heel and then the other, again slightly faster than his current rhythm.

Whichever aid you use, be sure to stop as soon as he begins to walk forward with energy. If he slows again, repeat the same ask-then-tell procedure. As he begins to understand, he should respond to your lighter request to avoid the harsher bump of your heels.

If you get no response to either your asking or telling aid, you may need to use a crop to tap his rump and make him move. Tap slightly faster than his current rhythm and cease tapping when he responds.

. . . to get the correct bend.

At the other extreme is the horse that refuses to walk, preferring instead to jig or jog. Here, every time that your horse begins to move faster than a walk, pull him into three tight, consecutive little circles. As you reach the point in the third circle where he will follow the straight-line path, relax your aids. This will give him a chance to walk straight forward in a relaxed gait. If he begins to jog after a few steps, immediately pull him into three more tight circles. Release the aids and let him walk on the straight-line path again. Stay quiet and relaxed for as many walking steps as he will give you, yet be sure to correct him immediately if he begins to jig.

If you *consistently* correct your horse in this manner, you will get more walking steps. Conversely, if you let the horse jig once and not the next, he will be confused and will not understand your correction and will continue to test you. Consistency is the key. You must correct him every time, *as soon as* he begins to go faster than a walk. He must understand that jigging or jogging are not acceptable and that he will get pulled into three little circles every time that he tries to go faster than a walk. Depending on how long your horse has had this problem, it can take one day to three months to correct. Don't get discouraged.

BEND CORRECTLY

When you reach the end of your arena walking a straight line, ask your horse to turn in a half-circle. To teach your horse to bend correctly, bend him around your inside leg as you lift your inside rein. Apply the neck-rein cue as well so that he associates the cue with turning. Keeping a rein in each hand allows you to lift the horse's inside shoulder in case he begins to fall into the circle.

If you are turning to the left, you will use left-leg pressure at the girth to bend the horse in an arc around your left leg. At the same time, to keep the horse from throwing his hip to the outside, put your right outside leg slightly behind the girth to keep the horse's hindquarters in the correct arc of the circle. Depending on the horse's level of training, you can use the neck rein alone, or you may need to help him with a direct rein as well.

The arc of the horse's body should match the arc of the circle. If you are making a small circle, the horse's body will be arced more than it will be on a larger circle. Vary the size of your half-turns to get the greatest benefit from this exercise. *Aim for correctness.* Be sure that the size of the circle is *your decision,* not the horse's.

When you use circles in your exercises, be sure you decide the size of the circle, not the horse.

If the horse falls into the circle, simply lift your inside rein to correct him. This will elevate the horse's inside shoulder. This will tell him to stay upright and balanced as he walks the half-circle. When you reach the end of the half-circle, release your turning aids and let the horse walk straight forward on this new path to the opposite end of the arena. Alternating half-circles first to the left and then to the right will establish the serpentine pattern that will progress the horse and rider down the length of the arena. The result should be *exact*, straight lines traversing the arena, connected by perfectly half-round half-circles. That is your goal. You should enter and exit each half-circle on a straight line and leave on a straight line. Each half-circle should be the same size as the previous one unless you purposely decide to change the size. Strive for a perfect pattern, because that is how both you and your horse will gain the most benefit.

INCREASE THE DEGREE OF DIFFICULTY

Once your horse can walk the serpentine pattern correctly, you can begin to increase the degree of difficulty. Instead of walking the straight-line segment of this exercise, begin to jog. When you are ten feet from where the horse must make his half-circle, bring him back to a walk. Walk the half-circle correctly. When he is straight and headed down the new straight-line path, ask him to jog again. The only differences are the increase in speed and the transitions from walk to jog and jog to walk.

When you feel comfortable with your horse's response, move on to the extended trot. This will help teach him speed control at the trot before you later teach it at the lope and gallop. Ask him to extend his trot on the straight line. Ten feet before you turn, ask him to walk and then walk the half-circle. As a variation, ask him to extend his trot across the arena, and then to jog the half-circle. Remember that the faster the gait and the bigger the horse, the more room he will need to circle correctly. Don't ask for more than he can physically give at this point in his training. Once your horse learns to collect and travel more under himself, your circles can get somewhat smaller, but don't ask for little circles until your horse is capable and ready to do so.

To keep your horse from anticipating, walk the half-circle one time and jog the next, jog two half-circles and walk three—anything to keep the horse guessing. Keep him paying attention to your aids and do not let him perform out of habit. Vary the pattern and your routine. You can make a full circle, or even two or three circles, at the point where you normally make the half-circle. Work on *correctness* and *obedience*.

When it feels like your horse understands and you are ready, lope the straight-line segment of the pattern, and then bring your horse back to a walk or a jog to make the half-circle. Then lope again. Perform walk-to-lope transitions or walk-to-jog transitions. Keep your horse alert and waiting for your command. Make him pay attention.

If you incorporate this serpentine exercise into your daily schooling, your horse should become

> **Be an active participant as you ride, not just a passenger.**

If your horse shows signs of resentment, you may be asking too much too soon. Or you may have to show the horse that you demand respect and obedience.

End your lesson when he is bending to the best of his ability.

more responsive to your aids. Remember to be an active participant as you ride, not just a passenger. Use lighter and lighter aids as you progress.

SIGNS OF RESENTMENT

If your horse starts to resist or shows signs of resentment during your lesson, you may be asking for too much, too soon. Try going back a step and working at the slower gaits until he shows signs of being more cooperative. Then try to increase the degree of difficulty again. Give him plenty of time to understand what it is that you want before you push for more.

Make sure that you end your lesson on a good note. This tells your horse that he must behave before he quits for the day. At the end of your schooling session, you can take your horse for a relaxing ten-minute walk, or you can dismount right there and put him up.

Spending ten minutes a day on this simple routine will help to progress your horse's training along the right path and should result in your horse becoming more responsive and lighter to your aids.

Always end your lesson on a good note.

CHAPTER ELEVEN

Teaching Leads and Lope Departures

TEACH IN STEPS

In just about every type of discipline, from reining and Western-pleasure classes to equitation or barrel racing, a horse must know how to depart from a walk to a lope on the correct lead. However, before you can teach a horse leads, you must be sure that he understands the concept of loping. It is only after a horse lopes consistently from your cue that you can teach him to lope on a specific lead.

Similarly, wait until after a horse consistently takes the correct lead before teaching him the walk-to-lope departure. If you try to teach the lope departure while you are teaching leads, you will only confuse the horse. For instance, if he correctly departs into a lope, yet takes the wrong lead, you will have to pull him back to a walk—in effect, punishing him. It will not be clear to him whether he is being punished for loping or for taking the wrong lead. Therefore, you must teach him to lope first, then to pick up leads, then to make the walk-to-lope departure, and finally, to make flying lead changes.

It is easier to teach a horse to lope on the correct lead in a round pen, an

Your horse must learn to lope before he can learn leads.

arena, or other level area with a fence. Train in a ring snaffle bit if possible, so that you can take hold of the horse's mouth as needed. If you have taught your horse to lope from a kissing sound while on the longe line, he should also lope under saddle when you make that same sound.

The cue that I use for the left-lead lope is pressure from my right (outside)

87

If he lopes from a kiss in the round pen, he should easily learn to lope from a kiss under saddle.

hind leg and outside front leg (the second beat). His inside front "leading" leg completes the third beat of the gait.

Time your request for a walk-to-lope departure with his inside (front) shoulder moving back. His next step will then be with his outside hind leg. By asking at the correct time, you have set up the horse to depart on the proper lead. If, when you are mounted, you can also ask him to lope when you see or feel his inside (front) shoulder move back, the horse will again be in the proper position to take the correct lead. In this way, he will not have to scramble to adjust his feet to depart correctly. A ground person can help by telling you when the inside shoulder moves back so that you may begin to develop the correct feel for timing.

heel, slightly behind the girth. Use the kiss in the initial stages of training to help the horse associate your heel cue with loping. When the horse is completely trained, you may choose to discontinue the sound cue. In the initial stages of training, however, combining the leg cue with the "kiss" makes it easier for the horse to understand that you want him to lope, especially if you taught him to lope from a kiss in the round pen.

Asking at the right time sets a horse up to depart on the correct lead.

TIMING THE CUE

Timing is important when asking a horse to lope on a particular lead. Watch your horse as he departs from a walk to a lope on a longe line. If he takes an incorrect lead while being longed, bring him right back to a walk and ask him to lope again. Now watch the sequence of the fall of his hooves as he begins to lope. His outside hind leg starts the three-beat lope, followed by his inside

LOPE ON A CORNER

Another method that will help your horse depart on the correct lead is to ask him to lope on a corner in a rectangular arena. Many horses will easily take the correct lead in the direction of a circle. Simply stated, bend or circle the horse to the left for a left lead, and vice versa. When a horse lopes off on the correct lead, sit quietly to reward him and let him lope for a circle or two around the pen. Then *gently* bring him back to a walk. Be careful not to pull harshly on the reins to stop him or he may think that you are punishing him.

Remember—this first lesson is only to teach leads. Once he knows his leads, you may work on the walk-to-lope transition. For now, do not confuse him, but try to make it easier for the horse by timing your cue.

CORRECT HIM IF HE IS WRONG

When your horse lopes off on the wrong lead, quickly bring him back to a walk. Combine this with a verbal correction, such as "quit" or "stop." "No" and "whoa!" are both one-syllable words that sound the same (to a horse) and often confuse him. It is not the specific word that you use as much as it is your tone of voice and using the same correction word consistently. The horse will soon learn that you will not accept him departing on the incorrect lead and that you will pull him back to a walk if he departs on the wrong lead.

To teach him why he is being corrected, you must *immediately* ask him to lope again (on the correct lead). When he ultimately departs on the cor-

rect lead, reward him by sitting quietly and letting him lope. If the horse takes the correct lead three or four times in a row, reverse and repeat the procedure on the other side. Always train on one side first before changing directions and working on the other side.

If a horse persists in taking the incorrect lead, he is telling you that he does not understand the cue to lope on that particular side. You must help him to understand that not only must he lope, but he must lope on a particular lead. He may become confused and refuse to lope. Don't be angry with him, because he doesn't understand.

HELP HIM TAKE THE CORRECT LEAD

To help your horse take the correct lead, first ask him to turn into the direction of the lead as you ask for a lope. For example, for a left lead, turn your horse to the left so that his body is arced to the left, or in a backwards "C," as you ask him to lope. Apply your right heel slightly behind the girth, and kiss

Push his hip to the inside. (I have exaggerated it here for emphasis.)

Then ask him to lope.

to ask him to lope as his left shoulder moves back, so his next step will be with his right hind foot, positioning him to depart correctly. If he takes the incorrect lead, pull him back to a walk. This time as you walk along the rail, lift your horse's outside (right) shoulder by lifting your right rein up. Try not to bend his nose out to the right. It should merely feel as if his right shoulder is elevated and his weight has transferred to the inside. Apply your right-leg cue, and kiss to ask for a lope.

If your horse still resists taking the requested lead, push his hip or hind end toward the inside of the rail. Keep light contact with both reins so that the horse cannot turn and duck back in the opposite direction or rush off when he feels your legs. Let him walk three or four steps with his front legs following the rail as his hind legs track to the inside. Then ask for the lope. His outside hind leg is now free to initiate the lope in the proper lope sequence. Again, ask as the inside shoulder moves back, so the outside hind leg can initiate the departure. For example, for a left-lead lope, use your right leg slightly behind the girth to push his hip to the left. Now, when his left shoulder blade moves back, cue for the lope. He should depart on the left lead.

> You must teach the horse that there is a specific cue for each lead and also that there is a reward for correct performance.

SIT QUIETLY WHEN HE IS CORRECT

Your horse should now lope off the left lead. When he does, sit quietly. Be sure that your reins are loose to reward him, and verbally praise him as you let him lope for two or three circles. You must convey to the horse that he is now

correct. Ease the horse back to a walk, and let him walk for a minute to reward him. Then, repeating the exact steps that caused him to take the correct lead previously, ask him to lope again. When he again takes the correct lead, reward him again as indicted above. After four or five times, either put him away for the day or work on something that is easy and does not involve lead work.

TEACHING A SPECIFIC CUE

You must teach the horse that there is a specific cue for each lead and that there is also a reward for correct performance. In order for a horse to learn the specific cues associated with each lead or gait, you'll need to invest time, patience, and consistency.

HANDLING REFUSALS

If your horse absolutely refuses to take a lead, look for a physical reason. For example, if your horse is sore on his left front leg, hoof, or shoulder, he will try to avoid taking a left-lead lope to keep the weight off that leg. If his body is not as supple on one side as it is on the other, he might also refuse to take a lead. Many horses are left- or right-"handed" and prefer one side over the other. In that case, build up his "bad," or less supple, side so that you spend maybe two-thirds of your riding time on that side. To help him gain condition and suppleness on his bad side, ask him to circle, stretch, and bend on his bad side. That might be all you need to do to help him learn to use both sides of

Lope in the round pen.

his body equally so that he will take either lead.

FEELING FOR THE CORRECT LEAD

The easiest method that I've found to teach a rider to learn to feel a lead (rather than *looking* to see if the lead is correct) is to go to the round pen—mounted—and lope your horse. First work to the left. Ask your horse to lope and have a ground person confirm that you are on the correct lead. Sit there quietly as your horse lopes. *Feel* how the left-lead lope feels. Then gently bring the horse back to walk and ask for a lope departure again. Feel how your body moves in rhythm with the horse when going to the left. Then switch sides and feel how your body feels when loping to the right.

When loping to the left on a left lead, you will feel the thrust of the beginning of the lope sequence. As mentioned earlier, a left lead lope begins with the outside (right) hind leg, followed by

The first beat of a right lead starts with the left hind leg. It is difficult for a horse to take the correct lead if he is not bent in the direction of the new lead. To understand this, sit on a chair. Bend your spine by bringing your right shoulder over towards your hip. Your left hip feels free, exactly as horse's does. It would be difficult for you to step off with your right (hind) leg because it feels weighted. It is easy to step off with your left (hind) leg and that is what a horse must do to begin a right-lead lope.

the inside (left) hind and outside (right) foreleg (the second beat), followed by the leading, left foreleg (the third beat).

When the horse brings his outside (right) hind leg forward to start the lope sequence, you will feel the thrust forward, or a bump, in the seat of your pants. Because the sequence starts with the right hind leg, you'll feel the first motion of the lope as a thrust on the right side of your seat. As you follow through with the rocking motion of the lope sequence, this initial thrust will be followed by the rocking motion of the lope and you'll roll to the left side of your seat; therefore, you'll know that you are on a left-lead lope.

If you are on the incorrect lead, the right in this example, you'll feel the first thrust on the left side of your seat and your body will roll to the right, or to the outside of the circle.

Loping in a round pen is beneficial for a couple of reasons. First, the horse will easily lope around the circle because of the smallness of a round pen. You will not need to guide him as you might in a bigger arena. Second, because his body is arced in the correct direction, he'll easily take the correct lead. (This is also an easy way to teach a horse to take leads.) And finally, because you do not need to guide your horse, you can concentrate solely on feeling the movement of a particular lead.

Your goal is to feel, rather than see, the correct lead.

ASKING AGAIN

Ask your horse to lope again. Feel the lead, lope two or three times around the pen and gently ring him back to a walk. Walk a circle or two and ask him to lope again. Have your ground person confirm each and every time that you are on the correct lead. If not, bring

your horse *sharply* back to a walk and *immediately* ask him to lope again, being sure you feel the incorrect lead.

Practice eight or ten departures on one lead and then switch to the opposite side and practice on the other lead. Practice eight or ten departures on this side and then take your horse and work on other maneuvers. If you do this consistently for a week or two, not only should you be able to feel what each lead feels like, your horse should be more solid or learn to depart correctly on whatever lead that you ask for.

Once you think you have mastered the techniques of feeling a lead in the round pen, then move to a bigger arena. See if you can feel a lead when your horse is traveling in a straight line. Again, ask your ground person to confirm that you are on the correct lead. Continue to practice until you don't have to look at the horse's shoulder to tell if you are correct or not.

TEACHING THE WALK-TO-LOPE DEPARTURE

Once your horse consistently departs on the correct lead, you can begin to teach the walk-to-lope departure. Set yourself up for success. Depending on your horse's ability, level of training, or response to your cues, you may ask for a lope departure on a corner or a straightaway. Try to put your horse in a situation where he will respond correctly (with the correct lead) in the initial stages of training. A word of advice—do not always ask for a lope departure at the same place, or you will be teaching a habit—not a cue.

To teach the walk-to-lope departure, make light contact with the horse's mouth as you ask him to walk. This will keep him from rushing off when he feels your legs. Squeeze both legs to "push him into the bridle," thus collecting and compressing his body. Hold him to a walk by restraining his forward energy with your hands. (Use the least amount of rein pressure needed to ask him to walk.) Because his body is compressed, he will feel like a coiled spring—full of energy. Ask him to lope by using your outside leg and the kiss cue. As soon as you feel him begin to lift off into a lope, loosen the reins and release him forward. He should depart directly from a walk to a lope.

If your horse jogs, rather than lopes, pull him right back to a walk to tell him that he did not perform the desired response. Repeat the walk-to-lope sequence, using a stronger cue to tell him to lope. This may either be a stronger bump from your leg or a tap from a crop. Again ask for a walk-to-lope transition. When he lopes, reward him by letting him lope around the arena on a loose rein.

> **Never practice a step repeatedly when the horse performs correctly.**

Then bring him gently back to a walk and ask him to lope again. If he tries to jog into the lope, pull him back to a walk. Then increase the severity of your cue to make him lope. Loping too fast is fine for now. You can always slow him down later, once he learns to lope directly from the walk.

When the horse does pick up a lope from the walk, be sure to sit quietly and allow him to lope on a loose rein for a couple of circles as a reward. Practice this four or five times, and then either stop for the day or do something unrelated to the work. Never practice a step repeatedly when he performs correctly or he may think he is being punished.

Push him into the bridle.

Then ask him to lope.

In subsequent sessions, continue to practice the sequence of cues that worked for your horse. Always use a cue consistently for each particular lead and let the horse lope for a few minutes to reward him. When your horse consistently takes the correct lead, you can begin to ask him to move away from leg pressure at the lope for a few strides in preparation for teaching him lead changes. After he understands the concept of moving away from pressure at a walk and jog, ask him to move away from leg pressure at the lope.

Training takes time. A horse must first learn the cue for a lead before you can teach him to depart from a walk to a lope. Once your horse consistently performs the proper lead on command, you can move on to teaching flying lead changes.

CHAPTER TWELVE

Teaching Circles and Speed Control

LOPING CIRCLES

If your horse lopes a perfectly round circle on your first try, congratulations! You have successfully taught him the basics of guiding. The easiest way to determine if you are riding perfectly round circles is to drag your arena or work area (or wait for rain to fall) so that the ground is clear of all old hoof marks. Then, lope your horse in a circle, making one circle to the left and then one to the right. Now look at the circle of hoof marks. Did your horse execute a perfectly round circle, or did he drift to one side or the other, making oblong, oval, or rectangular shaped circles? Did your horse try to drift or cut out to the gate? Did you feel that you had to guide him a bit more forcefully at one point or another? These are all clues that your horse needs more work on the basics of proper position. Riding circles should be part of your training routine and will give

If your horse lopes a perfectly round circle on your first try, congratulations.

you a good idea about the areas of control on which you need to work. Remember what your horse showed you on these test circles as you continue to train him.

BETWEEN THE BRIDLE

When your horse is loping a circle, he should remain upright and balanced,

Your horse must remain upright and balanced.

between the bridle, with his head slightly arced (looking) into the circle and his body or spine bent slightly around your inside leg. He should not veer or pull either to the left or to the right. He should stay on that same arced path of the circle until you tell him differently.

If you need help in guiding him in a correct circle, put a cone at each quarter of your circle and ride each quarter-circle from cone to cone. As you approach one cone, look to the next cone. (Looking to the inside or center of the circle will cause your horse to drift to the inside of your circle.) Guide your horse along the quarter-circle path and ride just to the outside of the cone. After riding round circles this way for a week or two, you will begin to feel what a round circle should ride and feel like. Then take away the cones. This is just one more way to get you started in the right direction.

Your body must be positioned correctly, and you must look where you are going. The angle of your body as you lope in a circle is one more cue to the horse to lope in a round circle. As you

Look where you are going.

look toward the next cone, your outside hip will be just a bit forward. Because of the position of your body, you can keep your rein hand above the horse's neck with the neck rein just touching the side of the horse's neck. While you may need to exaggerate your cues to the horse initially, perhaps helping your horse with a direct-rein cue from time to time, lifting a dropped shoulder, or using your leg to keep his body on the correct path of the circle, your goal is to have a horse that circles on a light cue.

FALLING INTO THE CIRCLE

If your horse drops his inside shoulder and falls into the circle, lift his inside shoulder with your inside rein. Lift him up, send him on, and then release the rein pressure. On occasion, a horse may drop his inside shoulder and then try to cut back into the circle quickly. Lift the inside rein to lift his inside shoulder and keep it lifted. Make the horse continue to lope. He may lope in smaller circles because of your lifted rein, but once he figures out that he must lope upright and balanced, he should lope correctly. Then release the rein and ask the horse to lope in the correct path of a circle. Remember—always lift the rein on the side of the horse on which he chooses to drop his shoulder, i.e., an inside rein for a dropped inside shoulder and an outside rein for a dropped outside shoulder.

DRIFTING

Does your horse start to drift toward the outside? Some horses will drift toward an open gate or toward the way out of your work area. If your horse starts to drop his outside shoulder, pick up your outside rein, gain light contact,

If your horse falls into the circle, lift his inside shoulder to pick him up and balance him.

then lift his shoulder to pick him up and balance him as you send him around the circle. Occasionally, with a horse that repeatedly tries to drop a shoulder and sneak off to the outside, you may need to gain light contact with that outside rein and then pop the rein upward once or twice as a correction. Correct him once or twice somewhat sharply. Don't nag or pick at him lightly, over and over again. Let him know that you mean it as a correction—that it is not something that he should try again. Then continue in your circle using the same form that you used prior to his drifting.

Nagging a horse by using little annoying tugs or tiny corrective measures can irritate a horse or turn the training session into a game. Correct once so that he understands that it was a correction, then go on. Some horses will pick a certain spot in your circle and will cut in or out at that same spot every time. You will often see them flick one or both ears back and forth right before they approach that spot. When the spot is close by, be prepared to give a correction. Correct your horse every time that he tries it for as many days as it takes to end this problem.

STAY UPRIGHT

Your horse must remain upright and evenly balanced between the bridle to perform the pretty, round circles on which you will score pluses. Your horse must remain upright and balanced when you ask for lead changes. If your horse drops his inside shoulder of the new lead when you ask him to change leads, he will, in all likelihood, change leads in front and drag or miss his lead behind. For your horse to slide to a stop correctly, his weight must be evenly balanced side to side. For him to perform a correct rollback, he must be balanced over his inside hind pivot leg so that he can elevate his front up and over his hocks to change directions. Correct him now every time that he drops a shoulder so that he learns

that dropping a shoulder is not acceptable.

WHEN TO USE ONE HAND, AND WHEN TO USE TWO

As you progress with your horse's training, if your horse will not guide by your neck-rein cue alone when you ask him to circle, you must work on correcting the error. Although I ride with two hands on the reins most of the time so that I can correct a horse, I ride with my hands close together. When the time comes to show him, he must guide with one hand on the reins. Riding with one hand on the reins is something that you must practice prior to showing. Practice riding one-handed at home so that both you and your horse are prepared at show time.

NECK REIN CORRECTLY

The correct way to neck rein a horse around a circle is to keep your

When using two hands keep them close together— preparing the horse for neck reining . . .

. . . so that transition to riding one-handed is easy.

hand *above* the horse's mane. Your rein will touch the horse's neck lightly on the opposite side from the direction in which you choose to go. For example, to circle to the left, your rein will be above the horse's mane and lightly touch the right side of the horse's neck. Pulling the neck rein over and down to the left side of the horse's neck will actually force him to tip his nose incorrectly to the right. The horse should follow his nose and bend his body in the correct arc of the circle.

If your horse tries to bend his head and neck into the turn but does not bend his body in the correct arc of the turn, lift your inside rein to straighten his head, use your inside leg at the girth to ask him to bend his spine around your leg and use your outside leg slightly behind the girth to keep the horse's hip in the correct arc of the circle.

Once a horse lopes in a circle with his body positioned correctly, you may ask him to gallop in large, fast circles. While you will not feel quite the degree of bend on a large circle, your horse must still look where he is going and keep his body in the correct arc of the larger circle.

Whether you are riding in large or small circles, be sure to vary the number of circles so that the horse does not begin to anticipate going across the center of the arena and changing directions with every circle. Vary the number of circles that you lope—maybe three in one direction, then six in the other. Walk a few circles, lope a few, then change directions. Vary the large and small circles so that the horse doesn't begin to anticipate always loping a certain number of circles and then crossing the arena. You must keep him waiting for your cues.

A quiet horse may take time to understand that he must extend himself and gallop. A quicker type of horse may need to gallop in many larger circles so

Keep your hand above the horse's neck. To gallop large, fast circles, I also bring my hand forward.

that he thinks of galloping as just one more thing that you ask him to do—something that he should do calmly. Horses need to learn to gallop correctly. It is not something that you can leave until the day of the show. Practice at home just as you do the rest of the maneuvers.

Ask your horse to lope in a large circle. To ask him to gallop, incline your upper body *slightly* forward and bring your rein hand slightly forward. At the same time, kiss to the horse to encourage him to go faster. Because he knows that the kiss is the verbal signal to speed up to a lope, he will increase his speed as you kiss to him to ask him to gallop. Be sure that your cues remain the same every time that you ask for an increase in speed from a lope to a gallop. This means that your hand always goes to the same forward position—exactly the same spot where it is now. Do not put your hand up to his ears one day and slightly above

Vary your routine to keep your horse alert for your cues.

Slowing after the gallop: Bring your hand back and sit deeper in the saddle.

the saddle horn the next day. Choose the spot where you are the most comfortable and use that spot consistently. On the same note, make sure that the angle of your upper body remains the same, day in and day out. Horses can feel the difference. For your horse to understand your body cues, he must be given them exactly the same way each time.

Once your horse is galloping, keep everything the same and encourage him to gallop. Let him learn that there is nothing to fear. Do not hit him with your reins or scare him in any way to make him gallop. This must be a controlled gallop, and for that to happen, your horse must be calm and in control. He must understand that these new cues are just another maneuver that he must learn. His speed will increase over time. Teach him to obey your cues first calmly and softly, then ease him up to a faster pace when he has shown you that he will obey readily.

When it feels like your horse wants to slow down, encourage him to gallop

for another minute, then sit more upright and look to the inside to prepare the horse to make a smaller circle off of the large circle on which he was just galloping. Simultaneously, relax your body, bring your rein hand back to its normal position, and guide him onto the track of the smaller circle. Making a smaller circle off of the track of the large circle will help to encourage the horse to lope slowly. A smaller circle encourages the horse to stay slow so that he can keep his balance and continue to lope.

If you let the horse continue on the larger galloping circle, he might confuse your body language of slowing to a lope with that of sliding to a stop. To execute a long, gliding, sliding stop, a horse has to increase his speed on his way to the stop. Increasing his speed encourages him to get his hind legs up under his belly so that he can then lock them in place as he elevates his shoulders and paddles in front. Guiding the horse off the track to a smaller circle is similar to what you will be asking him to do in a reining pattern; this will help him tell the difference between your body-language cues of slowing to a lope with sliding to a stop.

If your horse does not want to lope slowly, guide him into a smaller and smaller circle until he does slow down. Pulling or "hauling" on a horse's mouth will often just make him tough mouthed or angry. He must learn to lope slowly and in a relaxed manner. Continue around the smaller circles until he slows to the pace that you desire, then ease him back out into a loping circle. If he speeds up, decrease the size of your circles again. Small circles will naturally force a horse to go slower. A horse cannot keep his balance if he tries to race around a small circle. Using the smaller circle allows you to ask the horse to slow down naturally without pulling on his mouth. On some horses, this may take a week of loping in small circles; on others, it may take three months.

In addition to asking the horse to circle, I use my seat to tell the horse to relax. Open your hips, sink down into the saddle, let your legs relax on the horse's sides, and think "slow." Many horses will respond to this by relaxing and slowing their speed. If the horse's hind end is dragging out behind him, push it underneath him by taking a light hold on his mouth and asking him to collect—to drive his hindquarters up underneath himself. In this way, his stride will be more up and down rather than reaching forward. The tempo or beat stays the same, only the horse travels collected or more up and down.

Once your horse understands the concept of galloping and loping, lope for two or three circles, and then guide him to a large circle and ask him to gallop. Remember that the key to your horse learning lies in your providing consistent cues. Gallop a few circles, and then ask him to slow to a lope. If he does not follow through, ease him into smaller circles.

CONTROLLING SPEED

Besides riding in round circles, you must teach your horse speed control. Small circles in a reining pattern are loped slowly, while large circles are galloped.

Use Your Body Position

You can teach your horse to obey a slight shift in weight cue to slow down if you are consistent in the way in which you position your body. Your horse can differentiate your cues or your body position between loping fast and loping slow without the obvious signs of pulling back and hauling on his mouth. The less obvious your cues are throughout your pattern, the more polished and

professional you will look and the higher you will score.

Another advantage of teaching your horse to obey body position is that you do not have to rely solely on your reins. Some riders get show ring nerves and forget to move their hands *slowly* to signal a change in pace, causing a horse to open his mouth and toss his head. Sitting more upright in the saddle is an obvious signal to the horse that you want him to slow down to a "pleasure-horse" lope *if* you take the time to teach him that this is your cue to lope slowly. Inclining your upper body *slightly* forward with your rein hand *slightly* forward of its normal position over the horse's mane is an obvious signal to a horse that you want to gallop—*if* you ride this way consistently.

You do not want to change your position radically, because correct equitation is correct for a reason—it helps your horse do his job easily. Correct equitation is also *pretty*. It looks proper. Changing your position drastically calls attention to the fact that you are *cueing* your horse. The goal of good equitation is to cue your horse with aids that are almost invisible to a bystander. Ask your horse to gallop and to lope by using consistent cues, and your horse will begin to obey the slight change in position. Horses are much more aware of body position and body language than most people realize. Consistency is the key. If you do not ride the same way consistently, *every time* that you ask for a transition, how can a horse learn to obey this slight, yet obvious, signal? A horse will more readily obey your shift-in-weight cue once he realizes that by obeying this cue, you will not pull on his mouth.

Ride a Horseshoe Pattern

An exercise that I use often on all of my horses is to ride what I call a horseshoe pattern. Lope in a horseshoe (or upside-down "U"). As you come down the long end, or the right end, ask your horse to halt. Then turn 180 degrees, or one-half of a spin, to the outside towards the fence to change your direction. Ask your horse to depart immediately into the lope, and lope the pattern backwards, this time ending up on the left side. Do a 180-degree turn to the outside toward the fence and depart into a right-lead lope. You can vary the pattern by loping twice around the perimeter of the arena before asking for the next stop, or you can ask the horse to stop on the top of the arena (as if you were loping a U-shaped pattern). Change your pattern, and therefore his mind, by varying the distance to the end of the "U" before you stop, or else turn the pattern upside down.

This simple pattern provides many benefits. He'll practice spinning one-half of a circle, which will help his turn-arounds. It will improve his departures. Because he pivots around the inside hind leg, his next step is then with his outside hind leg which sets him up correctly for an inside lead. It teaches your horse to think slowly as he realizes that he'll be asked to stop at either end of the horseshoe. And it will help your horse to lope with his hind legs up underneath him, as he lopes the smaller half-circle.

Warm Him Up

Before you ask a horse to gallop, be sure that he is warmed up both physically and mentally. A horse can injure himself if his muscles and tendons are not warmed up slowly. It will take a heavily-muscled, stout horse as long as thirty minutes to get the blood pumping to all parts of his body. Give him time to stretch and prepare his muscles and tendons for more vigorous work and time to relax mentally. It might take some horses ten minutes to settle down and be ready mentally to learn; others

may take twenty or thirty minutes or even more. Know your horse and treat each horse as an individual. Suit your program to the horse, not the horse to the program. I let each horse walk on a loose rein for the first five minutes, then I go to a jog for another five minutes. I'll walk circles and serpentines, ask the horse to back up a few steps, move his hip to the left and to the right, and bend in either direction. Then, depending on the horse, I will let him lope a little or a lot. It depends on how fresh the horse feels that day.

Once the horse settles, I will bring him back to a walk to catch his breath and prepare him to work. I review briefly some of what the horse has learned in the past to put him in a working frame of mind. I might ask one horse to break at the poll and to jog or lope, or I'll go into jogging circles, stretching first one side of the horse and then the other. At the walk, I will ask a horse to bend and correctly arc his body to conform to the circle and then I'll ask him to hold that same bend or arc, yet travel in the opposite direction. For example, first ask your horse to circle to the left. Then, keeping everything the same (his head and spine bent left), ask him to make a right circle, by using your left leg to push him around a circle to the right. This is explained in more detail in the chapter on spinning. I will ask him to two track, or move laterally to the left and to the right, and then later to cross over and spin slowly first to the left and then to the right. Then, when the horse is settled and paying attention, I begin to teach him new things. A horse that has not yet settled down will find it almost impossible to concentrate on learning.

You can practice loping and galloping as part of your conditioning program, but be sure not to ask for more than your horse is capable of giving at that point in his fitness level.

Counterbend—Start by circling your horse to the right.

As you finish your circle . . .

. . . keep your inside right leg on his side.

Keeping the same bend in his body, use your right leg to push him left.

Keep his nose slightly tipped to the right.

Use your right leg . . .

. . . to push him left.

Conditioning takes time, and a horse must be brought up to peak condition slowly. And once a horse is at his optimum fitness level, he cannot stay there indefinitely. He needs periods of rest for his body and mind.

When the time comes to let a horse back down from his peak fitness level, do so in the opposite way from which you brought him up to it. Begin to decrease the amount of work and slowly let him down. When the time comes for his next peak, bring him slowly back to his maximum level until the time comes to let him down again. An equine athlete has much in common with a human athlete and should be treated with the same care and respect. Warming up and cooling down a horse properly will result in fewer stiff, pulled, or sore muscles. Your horse will stay sound longer and will have fewer days off if you treat him with the care and respect that he deserves.

CHAPTER THIRTEEN

Collecting The Horse

CAPTURING YOUR HORSE'S ENERGY

"Collection" is not only a fancy term and maneuver used by dressage people—it is something that all horses should be taught. Collection is taught by taking a light hold of your horse's face to capture the energy that is generated by his hindquarters. You do this by squeezing with your legs to force the horse up into the bridle. This teaches your horse to move with his hind legs up underneath himself, his head perpendicular to the ground, and his back rounded. In this position, your horse is physically prepared to perform whatever maneuver you might ask of him next. Collection not only teaches your horse to carry himself in a particular way, but it can be used to change the length of your horse's stride. While the tempo or beat stays the same, the horse moves more up and down when collected, as compared to reaching forward when strung out.

A horse that carries himself with his body strung out, his hind legs dragging, or his back hollowed and his head in the air is physically unable to perform all but the simplest of maneuvers—and even those may be difficult for him. A horse that does not carry himself properly, sometimes caused by lack of training or the horse's actual physical makeup, can develop sore muscles. When the horse resists, becomes resentful, or refuses to perform a certain maneuver, it may be caused by soreness rather than by your horse not trying.

When you ask a horse to collect, you drive his hindquarters further underneath him by using your legs— squeezing to tell him to go. At the same time, you keep a light hold of the reins to capture the energy generated by his hindquarters. This energy surges up to meet the barrier created by the bridle reins. Think of a slowly moving, closed door in front of the horse's face. A light hold of the reins causes that captured energy to make the horse stride more up and down, rather than reaching forward with each stride. If you take a slightly tighter hold of the reins with a highly trained horse— one that understands collection properly—he would move even more up and down, until finally he would trot in

> **A collected horse can perform manuevers safely and correctly.**

place—the piaffe. (A piaffe is a highly schooled dressage movement but it illustrates this point perfectly.)

Collection can be compared to the water behind a dam built of bricks. When the dam is fully in place and the water is rushing up it, the water rises higher and higher. There is no outlet for the energy created by the water. This would compare with the piaffe—the trot in place. When you remove a few bricks, the water is still high, although not quite as high as it was before you removed the bricks. Some of that water—or energy—is leaking out the front. The same is true of a highly collected trot. You release a little on the reins and allow the horse to move slightly forward, rather than straight up and down as in the piaffe. As you remove more bricks, the water gets somewhat lower—more water or energy is going out the "door" that you opened, although you have not yet let it release fully. This is your average collected trot. Finally, you take away all of the bricks and the water flows through the dam flatly, allowing little energy to be created by the water. This is similar to a horse performing an untrained jog. Although I have used the trot as my example, collection applies at the walk and the lope as well. While only a well-trained horse can perform the piaffe (do not go out and expect your horse to trot in place), this shows what collection can do.

ENGAGING THE HINDQUARTERS

A horse's hindquarters are his power source—the location of the energy. (Remember the illustration in the first chapter?) The hind end pushes the horse forward. The front legs help to pull the horse forward. Collection teaches a horse to engage his hindquarters and to bring his hind legs farther underneath himself. This rounds his back and positions his hind legs so that he can instantly perform any maneuver. He is physically in position to propel himself forward and to perform.

A simple way to determine the distribution of your horse's weight is to ask him to walk from a halt. Does he reach with a front leg to pull himself forward in order to begin the walk sequence, or does he push off with a hind leg? Which is better? Is it easier to push or to pull a wheelbarrow full of manure? Obviously, pushing it is easier.

Ask your horse to walk on a loose rein for a few minutes so that he is relaxed. Now ask him to lope. Does he trot a few steps or scramble into it? Does it feel as if he is falling into the lope? Now repeat the exercise, but first take a light hold of the horse's mouth and ask him to flex at the poll (and give to the bit) while you squeeze both legs. Squeezing your legs will send the energy of the horse to the bit, where this energy meets a slight resistance—namely, your light hold of the horse's mouth. This will cause him to collect or compress his body much like a coiled spring.

See how deeply this horse strides underneath himself after a year's training. Although I am not holding the reins to "capture his energy," through months of training he has learned to collect on a loose rein.

Now ask him to lope. You should get a nice departure into a balanced, even-strided lope. It should feel as if he is lifting or pushing off into the lope from his hind end rather than falling forward into it. A collected horse is prepared to do whatever you ask of him because his body is in the correct frame to respond.

Remember that collection starts with the hindquarters and carries through to the face. A horse can drop his head to a vertical position, yet still not be collected. A horse *can* travel with his hindquarters dragging behind when his head is in a vertical position. That is not collection. Collection starts at the hindquarters. Squeezing your legs creates energy—it signals "go" to a horse. Your hands capture that energy by taking a light hold of the horse's mouth and asking him to flex at the poll as he drives his hind legs farther underneath himself and rounds his back. When you hold a horse's face and squeeze your legs to create more energy, that energy starts at the horse's hindquarters, comes through the horse, and meets the resistance of the bit—back to front. In time, a horse will learn to hold this collected position on his own with a loose rein.

TEACHING TO FLEX AT THE POLL

By teaching a horse to flex at the poll from the bitting exercises on the ground (See Chapter 5), you teach a horse to give to the bit and flex at the poll in response to rein pressure. Working on the ground allows the horse to concentrate on the job at hand. There is not a person on his back who might send conflicting signals or in some way distract the horse. This frees the horse to decipher the proper response while he learns to give to the bit and understands that relief from pressure comes from backing off the bit. I find that

Ask the horse to collect at the trot.

Medium trot.

Extended trot—compare the length of stride.

longeing a horse with his head tied as described in Chapter 5 teaches him to give his head more quickly and saves me time, because I can then ride that horse and squeeze my legs and not get into a pulling contest with him. He has learned from his ground work that the only way to gain relief from bit pressure is to flex at the poll and drop his nose to a vertical position. Because the horse is soft in the bridle and easy to control, you can direct how much energy you have created by squeezing your legs to get the desired degree of collection.

Asking a horse to lope in a small circle when collected allows him to stay upright and balanced. Asking a horse to change leads when he is collected allows him to do so, hind end first, which is correct. His body is in a position that allows him to perform the lead change easily. When a horse is strung out or moving on his forehand, he will find it physically difficult to perform any but the simplest of maneuvers.

Flexing at the poll and using a lot of leg causes this horse to step deeply underneath himself with his inside hind leg.

TEACHING COLLECTION

When you begin to teach collection, your horse must first understand to flex or give to the bit in response to rein pressure. Rein pressure alone doesn't make a horse collect. If your horse understands to flex at the poll in response to rein pressure, he will not raise his head in the air or fight the bit when you take a light, even hold of the reins. To ask a horse for collection, you *must* take a light, even hold of the reins—to contain some of the energy created by your legs—while you simultaneously squeeze the horse up into the bridle with your legs. Your legs ask the horse to create energy—energy he would use to move forward faster if you allowed that energy to leak out the front. Your hands control the amount of energy that you allow the horse to use to go forward. In other words, rather than racing forward, as a horse might if you squeezed his sides to make him go, your hands on the reins ask him to flex at the poll and you allow him to move forward maybe half as much. Rather than reaching forward, the horse uses that energy to move more up and down—collection. Compare a race horse galloping, reaching forward with every stride, to a well-trained show horse that can lope upright and balanced in a small circle. The race horse's energy is used to cover ground. The well-trained show horse that lopes slowly in a small circle uses that same energy, but it causes him to move more up and down—again, collection.

To begin to teach collection, ride your horse in a snaffle bit if he is obedient in that type of bit. This way you can take hold of the reins to contain his forward energy without worrying about pulling on his mouth.

Ask your horse to trot. When he settles at the trot, take a light, even hold of his mouth to ask him to flex at the poll. At the same time, squeeze with your legs so that he does not confuse the rein signal to collect with a signal to halt or slow. With one horse, you may need only to squeeze lightly to indicate to the horse that you want him to trot but to trot collected. With a different horse, you might need to really squeeze him up into the bridle in the initial stages. If your horse is extremely quiet, and you have a secure lower leg, you might need to wear blunt spurs for awhile so that he understands that he must "go," even though you have hold of his face. Don't pull back on the reins. You should feel your horse flex, then keep your hands steady at the point where he is comfortably flexed. Don't pull—hold the reins steady. Your goal is to feel the horse's mouth through the reins which should be soft and elastic. Don't get into a pulling contest and *don't* let him pull the reins out of your hands! Just keep a nice, light hold to contain a bit of the energy generated by his hindquarters. Squeeze him up into

the bridle with your legs. As his head drops and he engages his hindquarters, you will feel his back round, or rise under your seat, as he shortens his stride. Hold him in this collected position for five or ten steps initially. Then release him and let him move out on a loose rein. Go once around the arena and ask again, then release and praise. Continue working this way for a week or so, then begin to ask him to hold that flexed, collected position for a longer period of time.

Once your horse has mastered the concept of flexing, engaging his hindquarters, and rounding his back at the trot, you may ask him to collect at a lope. Adding speed always increases the degree of difficulty. It is easier to teach a horse to collect at a trot and then teach him to collect at a lope. You may find it helpful to have the horse travel in smaller circles as you ask him to collect because these smaller circles will naturally force him to slow down and collect.

Release to tell him he did as requested and to reward.

To teach a horse to bridle up, or to give to the bit and flex at the poll, set your hand in one place (don't pull!) and use your legs to push the horse up into the bridle. Compare this to the photo on the previous page. You can almost see the energy in this photo.

This is a different horse, but again you can see the energy in this slow, collected lope. This is an old photo and the rings of the martingale are way too low—do not adjust them this low.

Remember that this exercise uses new muscles. Don't ask for too much initially. Gradually increasing the length of time that your horse holds a position will allow him to develop those muscles without getting sore or resentful.

Once the horse understands the concept of collection, incorporate periods of it into your daily work. Ask him—over weeks, not days—to hold the collection for longer periods of time. This will help your horse to better perform all maneuvers. Teaching collection will greatly benefit your horse when you begin to ask for lead changes. It will also help when you ask him to lope in a small circle, and it will help a horse depart into the lope. While you do not need to teach your reining horse to piaffe, teaching him to collect is one more way to develop control. Remember—the goal is to have a finished reining horse that shows little or no sign of resistance, and one that performs what you ask of him.

CHAPTER FOURTEEN

Making Smooth Lead Changes

A NATURAL SKILL

A horse is born knowing how to change leads and also how to perform a flying-lead change. Some horses are better and more graceful at changing leads than others, but all horses can change leads. Watch your horse as he gallops and plays in the pasture. Most horses at play change leads almost effortlessly when they change directions. The challenge is how to teach a horse to change leads on command.

When you first start working a colt in a round pen, he may show you if he wants to be on the correct lead, or if he is just as happy loping on the incorrect lead. Another colt may counter-canter—take one lead in front and the opposite lead behind—and lope around the pen, lap after lap, in that manner. A colt like this may not yet have the muscle strength to "hold" a lead and may only need time to muscle up or become more conditioned. Others that counter-canter often or that lope on the incorrect lead after a few months of conditioning do not naturally have good leads. A horse that consistently takes the correct lead or that changes leads so that he is on the correct lead will usually learn to change leads more easily than a horse that doesn't as you progress with your training.

BEFORE YOU ASK FOR A LEAD CHANGE

Before you ask a horse to change leads, you should understand the sequence of the horse's leg movements when he lopes on a particular lead. The lope is a three-beat gait that begins with the outside hind leg, followed by the outside foreleg and the inside hind leg—the second beat of the lope—followed by the inside front "leading" leg—the third beat of the lope. The horse's inside legs extend a little farther so that when the horse lopes in a circle, he can stay balanced. When a horse changes directions, such as when he is performing a figure-eight, he must change the pattern of the fall of his feet to begin the new lope sequence on the opposite lead. To do this, a horse can do a simple change of leads where he breaks to a walk or a jog at the center of the pen before picking up the new lead to lope in the opposite direction. Or he can perform what is called a flying-lead change.

In a flying-lead change, a horse must keep his shoulders elevated so that he can reach underneath with his "new" outside hind leg to change the pattern of his feet. For example, if the first circle of the figure-eight is loped to the right, the sequence of the right-lead lope would be: left hind leg followed by the second beat of the outside (left) front leg and the inside (right) hind leg, followed by the right front leading leg. When the horse crosses the center of the eight, he must change that pattern to a left-lead lope. Here the sequence is: right hind leg followed by the second beat of the inside (left) hind leg and outside (right) front leg, followed by the inside left leg. There is only a brief second, when the horse is finishing the lope stride, that a horse can change leads, or change the pattern of his hind legs, to begin the new lope sequence. This occurs when he is on the third or final beat of the lope sequence. His leading front leg is on the ground, and both of his hind legs are off the ground. Therefore, he can swing through with the new hind leg to create the new lead.

WATCH YOUR HORSE

Watch your horse at a lope while you longe him. As his inside front "leading" leg hits the ground, both hind legs are in the air for a split second. Now, your horse can bring the opposite hind leg forward to change his pattern and therefore his lead from back to front.

TEACHING THE CUE

Before you can teach the cue for a flying-lead change, your horse must understand and consistently lope on the correct lead from a given cue. He must understand that there is a cue for each lead so that he knows that you are asking him to *change* to the new lead when you *cue* for it. He should lift his shoulders in response to your rein cue with-

out becoming upset when you take hold of his mouth to lift his shoulders. A horse that is fighting a rein cue will put his head in the air, hollow his back, and be unable to perform the simplest of commands.

If a horse drops his shoulder going into the lead change, as he might do if you throw your weight in the direction of the new lead, he will most likely change leads in front but miss the lead change behind. When this happens, he will be on one lead in front and on the opposite lead in back. This is commonly called a cross-canter, which is very uncomfortable to ride. It feels as if the horse is disunited, which, in fact, he is. Some horses will cross-canter a few steps and then change behind, while others will stay in the cross-canter completely around the new circle. In either case, it is something that you want to avoid since you will lose points for cross-cantering. It is always easier to teach correctly from the start than to correct a bad habit. Try not to let your horse learn to change leads incorrectly; then you won't have to "fix" him later. A horse that "drags a lead"—or misses a lead behind—when he is asked to do a flying-lead change will get points taken off, as explained in Chapter 20.

A horse is born knowing how to change leads.

METHODS OF TEACHING LEAD CHANGES

There are different ways to teach the lead change. Some methods will work on one horse, while another horse may need a different approach. The technique that you choose will depend on your level of skill and on your horse's level of training and his natural ability. To teach a horse to change leads from your cue, lope in a pattern that resembles an "S." First lope in a medium-size circle to the left on the left lead at one end of your arena. To ride the "S," pick a point diagonally across the arena and lope in a straight line to that point. When your horse is traveling in a straight line, be sure that his right shoulder is elevated by lifting your right rein slightly, maintaining a light hold of your horse's mouth. The only time that a horse can change the pattern of his hind legs is at the end of the lope stride, when his leading front leg is on the ground. There is that brief second when both hind legs are in the air—that is the time to cue for the change. Keep his right shoulder elevated so that he cannot fall into the new lead, release your right leg, and cue him with your left leg. He should change leads. Ask the horse to finish the "S" pattern on the new right lead. You can also close the "S" and lope a small circle.

Do *not* throw your weight to the inside of the new circle, because this weights the front end of the horse, the opposite of what you need to do. A horse must be able to balance to change leads effortlessly, which means that you *must* stay centered and upright and balanced over the horse's spine. Don't bend his head in the new direction. Keep a light hold to keep that shoulder elevated, and release after he changes. The horse should be somewhat collected, allowing him that split second longer in the air. Collection shortens the horse's stride, making him travel more up and down and reaching under himself rather than strung out. If he doesn't change, do not punish him, because you will make him fear lead changes. He just does not understand yet. Try again, being more clear in your cues. Be absolutely sure that you do not lean forward!

TIME YOUR CUE

If you are unsure of the correct time to ask for the lead change, lope your horse in a circle as you relax and think only of the feel of the lope. Count: one, pause, two, three; one, pause, two, three, one, change. By saying the words, your timing should be correct. Also, as you lope, feel the effect each lead has on the position of your body. When a horse is on a left-lead lope, the right hind leg starts the sequence. Your right hip will roll forward slightly in front of your left hip and you will feel the lift off of the lope and bump or thrust on the right side of your seat. When you ask a horse to change leads, you must reposition your seat for the new lead. Look in the direction of the new lead. That will cause your left hip to be slightly ahead of your right hip, the correct position for a right-lead lope. As you cue with your left leg to ask for the change, changing from the right-lead to left as in this example, your hips will automatically change to the new lead position.

As your horse becomes proficient at changing leads in this manner, take your time. School for one or two changes in either direction, and then go on to something else. If your horse changes easily from one lead to the other, say the left to the right, school only on the opposite change for a few days. Once he changes leads easily, don't make him become resentful by changing leads over and over again. Teach him to change, but do not drill, drill, drill.

Also, be sure that he does not begin to anticipate the lead change. I spend more time teaching the horse to wait for my cue to

Teach, but do NOT drill, drill, drill.

The "S"—Start by making a left circle at the top of the arena. This horse is at the second beat of the lope. The outside foreleg and inside hind leg are both on the ground. The third beat will occur next when his inside foreleg touches the ground. That would be when to ask for a change.

As you come out of the circle, pick a diagonal point across the arena and travel straight towards it. Look up! Sit up!

He has changed to the new right lead and departs from the right hind leg for a left-lead lope.

Ask for a lead change in the middle of the "S." His next step will be the third beat with his left fore leading leg touching the ground. Ask for the change now—it is the only time he can change the pattern of his hind legs.

Finish the "S" on the new lead.

Another lead change—the horse changes the pattern of his hind feet. The thrust from his hind legs to begin the lope sequence has boosted me slightly forward, but try your best to stay upright and centered. Leaning forward makes it harder for your horse!

change than actually changing leads. Keep your horse honest and waiting for your cue by loping three circles in one direction before you ask for a change. Other times, lope a few circles, then stop in the center of the arena. Another time, ask him to counter-canter (canter on the incorrect lead) the new circle by keeping your leg on him on the side of the old lead. For example, if you have just loped a circle to the left, as you cross the center of the arena, keep your right leg on the horse to keep the left lead, as you guide him on a circle to the right. This is hard work for a horse. In most cases, loping one circle in a counter-canter, especially in the initial days of training, is sufficient.

CHANGE LEADS OVER A LOG

If your horse does not change leads, you can try two other methods. An old method, but one that is still ef-fective, is to place a ground pole at the point where you ask your horse to change leads. I suggest that you use the pole only long enough to teach your horse that this new cue tells him he must now change leads. Then re-move the log and ask him to change on your cue and body position alone. Think of using the pole as a step in teaching the lead change, just as you teach him to spin, one step at a time. This method not only helps the horse—by lifting his body in the air for a second longer as he goes over the pole, thus giving him more time to make the change—it is helpful to rid-ers who need to learn the correct feel of the timing of the change. As you feel the horse lift up to go over the log, ask him to change leads with *your* "new" outside leg. Then slightly change the horse's direction with your neck-rein cue, keep his shoulders ele-vated, and lope the new circle. Staying in the air for that second longer makes the switch of leads easier for him.

Change leads as you center over a log or pole. Do not lean forward as I'm doing here. Look up—that will keep your head and shoulders up!

The second method is using a slight variation of the "S" pattern. After loping the first circle, say to the left, bring the horse back to a walk at the center point in the straight-line segment, where you would otherwise ask for the change, then ask him to side pass for three steps to the left using your right leg to push him left. Immediately ask for a right-lead lope departure. When your horse has been walking in the center of the pattern for a few weeks, and you are sure that he readily understands and lopes off easily in the new lead, begin to eliminate one sideways step. This time, lope, walk, side pass for two steps, and lope off. After another week or two, eliminate another sideways step. Now the pattern becomes lope, walk, side pass one step, and lope off. The next step is to ask for the flying-lead change without breaking back to a walk.

Another variation is to lope a medium-size circle to the left on the left lead at one end of your arena. As you ap-

proach the far corner, or the bottom of the "S," pick a point diagonally across the arena and lope in a straight line to that point. When your horse is traveling in a straight line, be sure that his right shoulder is elevated by lifting your right rein slightly, keeping a light hold of your horse's mouth. Take your right leg and push the horse to the left, still at a lope. This will bend his body in the correct arc of a right-lead lope while you move, or counterbend, to the left. Ask your horse to move to the left, while his body is arced to the right, for three to five strides. The only time that a horse can change the pattern of his hind legs is at the end of the lope stride, when his leading front leg is on the ground. There is that brief second when both hind legs are in the air—that is the time to cue for the change. Keep his right shoulder elevated so that he cannot fall into the new lead. Then release your right leg, and cue him with your left leg; he should change leads. Ask the horse to finish the "S" pattern on the new right lead.

VARY THE LOCATION WHERE YOU ASK FOR A CHANGE

Be careful not to ask a horse to change leads in the same place every time. He will begin to think of that area as the place to change leads, rather than waiting for and learning your cue. Changing in the same area may be helpful for a week or two, but then begin to vary your routine. Lope three or four circles on the left lead before going into the "S" pattern and asking for a change. Counter-canter a circle without asking for a change of leads. Lope three circles to the left, stop, then lope five circles to the right. Ask your horse to change leads, then bring him back to a halt. Use your reins very gently to signal the halt to prevent him from thinking that you are correcting him for changing leads by pulling on his mouth. Always think of the message you may be sending to the horse. Stop him, sit on his back, and let him rest for three or four minutes. This is a good cure for a horse that wants to rush through his lead changes "to get them over with."

Always vary the place in the arena where you ask for a change.

WHEN A HORSE GETS RESENTFUL

If a horse begins to pin his ears or kick out after a lead change, think of what you may have done to make him resentful. Have you schooled too often on lead changes? Have you hooked him with a spur? Is he sore anywhere? If your horse begins to resent changing leads, keep your schooling of them to a minimum. Reward him by dismounting right after the change and put him up, or sit on his back, let him rest, and go on to something else. A horse should change leads as easily with you on his back as he does when free in a pasture. To keep your horse performing with a good attitude, you must *work* at keeping it that way. If a horse changes correctly for a period of time but then becomes resentful, think about what message you may have inadvertently sent to him to make him so cranky.

CHAPTER FIFTEEN

Teaching Your Horse to Spin

AGAIN, TEACH IN STEPS

Before a horse can learn to spin, he must understand the cue to move away from leg pressure and he must know how to neck rein. He must also be able to elevate his shoulders in response to the lifting of the reins. In order to achieve the high-speed spin seen in today's competitive showing world, the horse must learn to move his inside front leg back and out of the way to make room for his outside front leg to cross over. This creates the front part of the spin. As he learns to plant his inside hind pivot leg, which supports his weight throughout the spin, he pushes with his outside hind leg and pulls with his outside front leg, drawing his body around the turn.

The spin is not a natural movement for a horse to make. You must teach your horse to spin in a logical succession of cues, so he learns the correct form before you add speed. Slow, correct form should always be scored higher than incorrect form with speed. With this slow, correct, gradual teaching, your horse will not hop around his spins and fail to plant his pivot foot, enabling him to spin in place. Pushing for speed too soon can result in your horse not learning to back his inside shoulder out of the way, thus hitting his inside foreleg when his outside leg crosses over. As a result, he will hop or bounce around his spins, rather than cross over correctly and stay flat.

The speed in a spin comes from the forward motion that is created by the impulsion from the horse's hindquarters. The hindquarters are the horse's engine. He uses his *outside hind leg* to push himself around the turn as his *outside front leg* helps pull his front end around, thus creating the spin.

TEACHING THE SPIN

To teach this magnificent maneuver, ask your horse to circle. On a young horse, I spend two to three months just making small circles—nothing fancier than picking up light contact with my inside direct rein as I ask the horse to bend around my inside leg; then I release the rein pressure. Pick up contact, bend, and release; pick up contact, bend, and release. Avoid pulling the horse around the entire circle with your direct rein, because you want him to remain light. You want him to think and

Look at the bulging hind end muscles as he spins.

to understand the cue rather than be forced to circle because his mouth is being pulled around to your knee. As the horse is circling from the direct rein, also place the neck rein on his neck so that later you can rely on the neck-rein cue alone.

For these initial circles, your outside leg just lies on his side, unless your horse begins to lag. Then, use your outside leg to bump him and create energy. Your inside leg is at the girth with light pressure. After bending the horse around your leg for three to four circles, release your cues and let him walk forward out of the circle—his reward for circling properly. When he understands how to circle in these small, walking circles, lock your elbow on your side and use only your forearm in an upward motion to lift his shoulder as you also direct rein him around the circle. This helps keep your rein cue light and keeps your horse from falling into the circle or dropping his shoulder into the turn.

TIME TO MOVE ON

Your horse will show or tell you, by his acceptance and understanding of the previous circles, that he is ready to move on. After countless sets of three to four circles in either direction, over the course of weeks or even months, your horse will begin to hold the bend from your leg cue alone for at least part of the circle. This is the reason why you pick up his shoulder, bend him around part of the circle, and release; pick up, bend, and release. The cues used in that manner force the horse to think. As you feel his response improving, you will know that he is beginning to understand. He realizes that if he tries to walk out of the circle prior to your release of the cues that send him forward, you will pick up contact and bend him again. Eventually, he learns to hold the bend from your leg cue alone. He learns that if he holds the bend, you will not use your direct rein and pull on his mouth.

RESISTANCE PROBLEMS

If your horse shows signs of resistance, you can pull him into a couple of tight circles with your inside direct rein. When he gives in and bends his body correctly around your leg, loosen your rein to reward him and let him walk forward out of the circle. Some horses may need to fight for a moment and will then give in and circle correctly; with others, resistance may indicate that your horse has a physical problem or that you have pushed for too much, too soon.

Anytime you run into a problem, try to rule out a physical cause first. Check for wolf teeth if your horse has a bitting problem or if he will turn only to one side and not the other. You may also notice your horse raising his head or opening his mouth uncomfortably when you put the bit into his mouth or

Ask the horse to circle—teach him to back his inside shoulder out of the way.

Pick up contact, bend, and release.

Elevate his shoulders.

Use right leg pressure tell him to begin to spin (to the left).

Elevate the horse's shoulders. Use your left leg to spin to the right.

He will learn to plant his right hind pivot foot.

as soon as you pull on a rein. Wolf teeth can be removed, and your horse will be much more comfortable and accommodating once he realizes the pain is gone. If a horse turns to one side better than the other, it may indicate that he is more one-sided. In this case, try to work more on his bad side, but also remember to work his good side by walking and jogging medium-sized circles. He will need time for his bad side to catch up to his good one. A slight lameness or soreness on one side or the other can also interfere with his training. This must be corrected before you can expect a horse to give you his best.

TEACHING THE ACTUAL SPIN

When the horse has shown you that he is ready to move on, you can begin to teach the actual crossover of his front legs—the beginning of the spin. Keep one rein in each hand and begin to walk the horse in small, walking-size circles, just as you did before. As you draw the circle down to where your horse is almost walking in place, take a light hold of his mouth with both reins to stop his forward motion and elevate his shoulders—you want to change the forward motion to the sideways motion of the actual spin.

Drop your weight to the back of the saddle—another cue to the horse that you now want to spin. Take your inside leg totally off his side, and at the same time, put your outside leg against his side. This is the cue to spin—the one that tells him to move sideways and away from leg pressure. Add your neck-rein cue, but be sure that your rein is above his mane, not down and over or on the side of his neck. This directs his front end around sideways to spin. Help him with a direct-rein cue, if necessary. Keep a somewhat snug hold of the neck rein so that it keeps the horse's head in a straight-forward position or in line with his body, but don't pull so hard that you tip his nose in the opposite direction in which you wish to spin. His body must remain straight and correctly aligned from head to tail.

Continue to lightly hold both reins up to elevate the horse's shoulders and to tell him that he cannot walk forward out of the spin. When he shows that he understands, you will discontinue this additional cue, but in the beginning stages, it helps the horse to elevate his shoulders and drop his weight back over his hocks. Your body should stay balanced and upright, not leaning either to the left or to the right. Sit with more weight on your inside seat bone, exactly as you do when you ask the horse to move in a small circle. Lean back, or bring your weight back somewhat, so that you help the horse put his weight over his hocks, allowing him to elevate his shoulders and cross over in front. If you lean to the left or right, or look down, you will unbalance the horse. Think of a child on your shoulders that cannot sit still. Isn't it hard to stay balanced? Your horse feels the same way if you shift your weight around as he is trying to learn, and later perform, the spin.

TAKE ONE STEP AT A TIME

The horse will start to take one and then two crossover steps with his front leg. As soon as he does this, let him walk forward out of the spin on a loose rein with your legs and all cues relaxed. Really praise the horse to tell him that he did what you were asking. And that is the beginning of a spin! Walk forward for ten to twenty feet and repeat the sequence. Reward the horse again as you let him walk forward out of the spin.

Walk forward ten to twenty feet and repeat, then praise again.

Walk around your arena on a loose rein a time or two and repeat the sequence, but on the other side. Go on to something else for five or ten minutes. Then repeat three sets of as many crossover steps as the horse will give at that point in time, first on one side and then on the other. Work first to the left and then to the right. Don't switch back and forth between sides in the initial training. Keep his mind on the left, do three sets of spin steps to the left, then go to the other side. That is enough for the first day. Ask the same way on each successive day. Intersperse this training with other activities to keep your horse from becoming bored.

As your horse progresses, he will take one crossover step, then two, then three, and so on. Ask for only a step or two initially until you feel his understanding of this new cue. Then ask for a little more. Soon you will get him to crossover correctly for a quarter-circle, and then a half circle. At this point, you can try to release the rein pressure that elevates his shoulders and use only the neck-rein cue. Remember, he must stay correctly aligned from head to tail. Be sure that your weight is back in the saddle to help him lighten his front and elevate his shoulders as he puts his weight over his hocks. In time, he will cross over correctly for three-quarters of a circle and then finally a full one.

Occasionally, you may need to show the horse what you want, perhaps by taking hold of his mouth, even backing him a step or two, if he continues to walk forward out of a spin. Asking in a corner and using the fence to stop his forward motion will also help. In time, he will learn to plant his inside hind pivot foot and pivot around that. Don't worry at these initial stages of training if he takes a step forward with that hind leg from time to time to catch his bal-

The horse must reposition his pivot foot throughout the turn.

Keep your weight slightly back to lighten his front end and as an additional cue.

Beginning to cross over . . .

. . . with the right front.

He takes another step . . .

. . . and crosses over again. When he understands the maneuver, release your reins even more to allow him to flatten out and really spin. As he gains in speed, he must have freedom of his head and neck to balance as he turns around or spins.

ance. He must learn to hold the position and must build up the muscles that allow him to do so.

If your horse tries to cross over with his outside front leg *behind* the inside front leg, *push him forward*. He needs more energy. He must learn that to spin correctly, his outside crossover foot must cross over *in front* of the inside front foot, *not behind* it. He must learn to back his inside shoulder out of the way for this to happen, especially at speed. Backing his shoulder out of the way is discussed in Chapter 9.

PROBLEMS

Remember that the spin is a forward-motion maneuver that is, in effect, a sideways motion—*never* is it a backward motion. If you get no response from your horse, he may not yet understand your rein cues or how to move away from leg pressure. Go back a step and work on those basic maneuvers before trying again. If, after teaching the horse to bend, to hold the small walking circles, and to move from leg pressure, you do not get a crossover step, perhaps you did not use enough rein pressure to keep him from walking forward out of the spin. Remember to also use your reins to lift the horse, elevating his shoulders while keeping your weight to the back of the saddle to help him lighten his front end and put his weight over his hocks. This allows him to take those beginning crossover steps. You may need to take a somewhat tighter hold of his head if he tries to walk through your reins or out of the spin, or you may need to bump him with your outside leg a time or two so that he pays attention to you and increases his energy level.

Because each horse is different and each rider is a bit different, you need to know your horse. Only *you* will know

Incorrect position—the rein hand is too far back, pulling the horse's head left while trying to neck rein right.

Here, the rider's hand is back and pulling on the horse's mouth.

See what happens when you release the horse's head.

When a horse has not learned to back the inside shoulder out of the way, he will bump his knees together.

The horse must learn to cross his outside leg over in front of his inside leg, not behind it.

how much leg or rein pressure it takes for your horse to respond. Play with varying amounts of pressure, always starting with the lightest amount first and increasing it as necessary. Be sure to sit balanced with your own shoulders upright. Check to see that the weight of your seat is balanced evenly from side to side. Don't look to the left or to the right, because the movement will shift your weight more to one side. And don't look down, because you will weight the horse's front end when he needs to have his front elevated.

If you use the neck-rein cue harder to try to make the horse turn faster, you will actually pull his head in the opposite direction from where it needs to be. The horse will be thrown off-balance, and he will be unable to spin in the correct form, if at all. As you teach this maneuver, the horse's head may be slightly bent into the direction of the spin, but it should never be pulled in the opposite direction from that in which you choose to go. As your horse begins to understand the maneuver, begin to decrease the amount of rein pressure (again, aiming for the lightest cue possible) and relying on leg pressure to tell him to continue the spin.

Even as the horse shows that he understands the cue to spin, keep it slow and let him walk one step at a time. You will begin to feel an even cadence to his step, a definite crossover-and-step, crossover-and-step rhythm. That is your goal at this stage in training. It may not feel like a fancy, show-stopping spin now, but by teaching the correct form, you are laying the foundation for correct form and speed later. When you consistently feel an even cadence to his step, then you may begin to ask for a little more speed. A cluck or a kiss may be all that is needed for your horse to move faster, or you may need to pop him on the butt.

If your horse starts to hop or bounce, however, slow him down and go back to even, cadenced steps. Don't be in a hurry to get to a fast spin. Correct form, with speed, will come, but only if you perfect the correct form first. If you watch a reining event, slow and correct should always be scored higher than fast and incorrect. Slow and correct may not get you any pluses in that segment of your run, but it will not deduct any points either.

THE FINISHED SPIN

Once your horse knows how to spin and you are ready to ask for speed, use the first quarter or half of your spin to tell the horse, "Yes, I want you to spin." That part of the circle sets the horse in motion, going around rather than forward. Be careful—make your cues distinct so that the horse does not confuse them with other cues. Start the spin slowly and work up to speed. As he settles into the spin, begin to kiss just

A more advanced horse. Notice that my weight is back to lighten his front end.

He takes a big crossover step. His body is straight head to tail.

Look at the size of the step.

In preparation for spinning with one hand on the reins, keep both hands close together so the horse learns the feel of the reins when used in this way. The reins and his tail fly as we pick up speed. My reins are loose to allow him to use his head and neck to balance with.

slightly faster than his rhythm. That will ask him to stay in rhythm but at a slightly faster pace. Vary the amount of your rotations during training so that he does not anticipate shutting down or stopping the maneuver after four spins every time. Use the last half of your last circle to prepare to stop. To stop spinning, release all cues and say whoa or slightly lift your reins as his signal to halt. Release all pressure when the horse does stop, to reward him.

A horse cannot learn to spin overnight, or even in a week or a month or two. You must put in those hours in the saddle, asking and showing over and over again without drilling your horse to death. Ask your horse at different areas of your arena so that he does not learn to anticipate spinning at one particular point. Walk around your arena

and ask your horse to cross over and spin for a half-circle so that he then faces in the opposite direction. Walk around a bit more and ask him to spin for a circle and a half. Be sure to praise him for good behavior so that he understands that he is performing correctly. A pat on the neck or a kind word can help keep your horse interested and wanting to learn. Remember to work both sides of the horse and to work more on the bad side if you find a problem.

ADDING SPEED

When you add speed to the spin, it is doubly important that you stay upright and balanced. You must do this to enable your horse to perform this maneuver. Think of spinning a top on the floor when you were a child. The least little push when it was spinning in place would send it off, rocking from side to side in a crazy fashion. Or think of the child sitting on your shoulders. When he wiggles from side to side, it is almost impossible to walk straight forward. When he leans to the left, your body naturally veers to the left. Think of what your body will do to a horse that is trying to spin in place if you are rocking or swaying from side to side. If you expect your horse to perform to the best of his ability, you must help him all that you can by gaining the strength in your muscles to hold your body centered so that he can spin in place.

TROUBLESHOOTING THE SPIN

A horse that doesn't plant his inside hind pivot foot will often try to swap end for end rather than spin around that locked-in-place pivot foot. A horse that is pushed for speed too soon—before he has learned to back his inside shoulder out of the way so that his outside front leg has room to cross over—will hop or bounce around the spin. Other horses will bang their knees together rather than back the inside shoulder out of the way. And still others have not learned to hold their weight back over their hocks and may try to walk out of a spin. All these horses must learn to elevate *both* shoulders so that they can put their weight back over their hocks to execute the spin.

While these problems require a rider who can *feel* when the offending maneuver is occurring and therefore correct the horse *at that time in the maneuver,* they are not insurmountable problems. Remember, a horse must learn how to spin slowly, step-by-step, before you can add speed to the maneuver. Only after a horse has learned how to spin, and knows where to put his feet, shoulders and legs, can you ask for speed. When you run into a problem, the answer lies in going back to the basics. In this case, you must go back to the slow crossover and step, crossover and step, "spinning" one step at a time.

Let's take these problems one at a time, starting with the horse that tries to spin quickly yet swaps end for end. The first step is to realize that, although it may look impressive to the uneducated eye (because of the speed with which such a horse can turn around), it is not the proper way to spin. Therefore you should see a penalty or minus on the score of your spins.

To have a visual picture of what the horse does when he tries to spin in this manner, picture a pole running through his center, much like a merry-go-round horse. If you push the back of a merry-go-round horse (and it was free to spin) it would ro-

tate round and round the pole. This is quite similar to what your horse does. However, to spin correctly, he must *plant* his inside hind, or pivot, foot, and sweep his body—which remains straight from head to tail—around that leg.

The first thing you will feel is your horse's hind end moving to the left (when spinning right). You must *stop* him. The stop says to the horse, "No! No! No! That is wrong. I don't want you to spin like that. That is incorrect." Then *immediately* tell the horse to back up as you lift his head, thus elevating his shoulders and sending his weight to the rear. Backing will get his weight over his hocks. If you expect this problem, be prepared. Ride with a rein in each hand. (I generally train with a rein in each hand, held closely together, in order to be better able to control my horse's front end.)

Tell the horse to back for three or four steps—just enough to stop the forward motion of the spin and get his weight back over his hocks where it belongs. Then, so that he understands what the correction was for, *immediately* ask him to cross over and spin, step by step, in *the same direction* that he was spinning before you corrected him. Because a horse must first learn on the left and then on the right, you must be sure to work on one side and then go to the other side.

Spinning slowly, step by step, allows you to feel when your horse begins to throw his hip to the outside, or when he begins to swap end for end. You must stop him when he takes that first wrong step (swapping ends) so that he understands exactly why he is being stopped and thus corrected. Back three or four steps to position the horse's

The spin must be taught slowly, step by step.

weight back over his hocks and to tell him that he was performing incorrectly. Then ask him to spin (in the same direction) cueing with your outside leg and using your inside rein to "pull" his head and front end around the turn. Your outside rein remains somewhat snug so that the horse can't bend his head and neck and remains straight from head to tail. If you know that he begins to swap end for end after one half of a circle (spin), stop him at three-eighths of a circle, just before he would take that wrong step. Then praise him. The praise tells him he responded correctly. *You can praise him because you stopped him before he could take a wrong step. Therefore, he spun correctly* (for as far as he got before you stopped him). A quarter circle spun correctly is better than a half a circle spun incorrectly. With a correct quarter circle, we can add one step at a time, day after day, or week after week, until you eventually get a correct full circle. From one correct circle, you can get two circles, then three and finally four.

If, after a few days, you feel no improvement, add this to the correction: when he begins to throw his hip to the outside, push (not jab) your spur into his side behind the girth to hold his hip in correct alignment. For example, if when spinning to the right, your horse tries to throw his hip out to the left, put your left spur into his left side behind the girth to tell him not to throw his hip to the outside. Your spur blocks his hip from swinging to the left. Ask him to spin again with your spur holding his hip from being thrown to the outside. If he stays in correct form, stop him gently and praise him. Repeat.

Always reward a good maneuver so that your horse understands what it is that you are looking for. A properly timed reward (when the horse is responding correctly) tells the horse he did as you asked. After enough rewards, he will want to repeat the behavior for which he was rewarded. That is the basis for all training.

Teaching Proper Body Position

Sometimes a horse has not yet learned to hold his weight back over his hocks. He may try to walk out of a spin. Lifting the horse's shoulders and backing him for a few steps as a correction, just as he *begins* to walk out of the spin, should teach him that walking out of the spin is not acceptable.

Another problem that sometimes occurs when we ask a horse to spin is when the horse's outside front leg does not cross *over* the inside front leg. There are several reasons for this. He may not have learned to lift and back his inside shoulder out of the way to make room for his outside (foreleg) to cross in front of his inside foreleg. An easy way to teach this is to teach the cue to lift a shoulder. Lift the rein closest to the fence to lift and turn the horse into the fence. Because of this proximity to the fence, the horse must naturally lift and then back his inside shoulder out of the way. This makes room for his outside leg to cross over and make the turn to go in the other direction. Use your outside leg to push the horse around the turn, just as you would for a spin, in effect asking him to move away from leg pressure.

Another exercise that I use to help with spin problems is the bend and counterbend exercise. Ask the horse to walk a small circle to the right with his entire body arced to the right, to match the size of the circle. Then, still keeping his head tipped to the right, and keeping the same arc in his body, push him to the left with your right leg. His body will still be arced to the right, like a "C", yet he will make a circle to the left, or counterbend. Make the circle to the right, keep the same arc, and counterbend a circle to the left. Release the horse's head, walk forward ten or twenty feet and repeat on the opposite side. Circle to the left, keep the arc, then counterbend a circle to the right. This is hard work, so don't drill on it.

If your horse still has problems spinning, try to feel if his inside front leg is carrying all the weight of his front end. He will feel "tipped" in that direction. Again, he *must* learn to put his weight back over his hocks. That is how he frees his front end to lift and cross over in the spin. If you have a good feel of the timing of a spin, you can lift that inside, weighted shoulder by lifting up the rein on that side. Step, lift up, step, lift up, and so on. As the horse understands that he is to put his weight back over his hocks and lighten his front end, it will be easier for him to spin.

Rider Error

While many spin problems are caused by a horse's error, or a horse's misunderstanding of a cue, rider error can play a part too. If you apply the neck rein too hard, it pulls your horse's nose in the opposite direction from that in which he is spinning. If you find yourself doing this, go back to using two hands on the reins for a while. Keep your hands close together, which will simulate one-handed riding to the horse; it therefore won't be a drastic switch when you go back to using one hand on the reins. Lay the neck rein against the horse's neck, keeping both of your hands in front of the saddle horn. Be sure that your neck rein hand doesn't cross over the horse's mane. A horse must be aligned from head to tail to spin correctly. However, if your horse tries to bend his head and neck in the direction of the spin, then you must

take a light hold of the outside rein and hold it somewhat snugly. Holding your neck rein snugly (without pulling the horse's head in the opposite direction) will keep his head and neck from bending into the spin, and his body aligned from head to tail.

If you hold your reins in your left hand while riding one-handed and your horse spins correctly to the right yet falls apart going to the left (or vice versa), this can also be a rider problem. When you ask your horse to spin to the right, your left arm is blocked by your rib cage. Therefore, your left hand seldom crosses the horse's neck so much that you pull the reins down and over his mane when going to the right. However, when you ask the horse to spin to the left, your rein hand and arm is free to move far to the left. If you pull on the neck rein trying to force the horse to move more quickly, you'll create problems.

In this example, because your arm is blocked by your rib cage when going to the right, your horse can spin correctly. So if you will lock your arm, from your elbow to your shoulder, against your rib cage when neck reining to the left, your horse's spins will improve. *You cannot force a horse to move faster by pulling on the neck rein.*

If your horse has been spinning incorrectly for a long period of time, you may need to use any or all of these corrections to fix the spin. It can be slow going for a while. Be patient. Teaching your horse the correct form of a spin before you add speed should make it easier for you to define and correct any mistakes that your horse might make. Once both you and your horse understand how to spin, then you can go ahead and kiss just slightly faster than

> **In order to spin correctly, a horse must be aligned from head to tail.**

his current rhythm to ask him to pick up and spin a bit quicker. Anytime you run into problems, back up a step and slow the horse down. Ask him to cross over and step, cross over and step. Look or feel for the problem. Aim for correctness. Think, what part of my horse is moving incorrectly? Am I cueing him wrong? How can I correct this? Then choose the correction that best tells him what it is that you wish to fix.

Remember, never be in a hurry to do the fast spins. You must first lay a solid base of training for the horse. Only then can you ask for speed in a spin. Given enough time and training, your horse will perform a properly executed spin with blazing speed—a spin that is low, fluid and fast.

CHAPTER SIXTEEN

Teaching Your Horse to Roll Back

EVALUATE USING THE ROLLBACK

You can evaluate a future reining horse's athletic ability by asking a young horse to perform a rollback while free longeing in the round pen. This will give you the chance to see how the horse uses himself naturally. The rollback is a 180-degree turn that a horse makes in place over his hocks, planting his inside, hind, pivot leg.

To perform a rollback, a horse must reach farther under himself with his inside hind leg and elevate his shoulders so that he can pivot over and around his inside hind leg. Teaching the rollback will help a horse later with sliding stops. This rollback maneuver teaches a horse where to put his hind legs—namely, right underneath himself, where they also must be to slide to a stop.

TEACHING THE ROLLBACK

Begin teaching this maneuver by free longeing your horse in the round pen. This will let him learn to handle himself unencumbered by the weight of a rider. Allow him to trot around the pen. Be sure not to restrict his head in any way. This is *not* the time to work on

setting his head or to have his head tied.

After he has warmed up and trotted around the pen a few times, take a step forward toward his shoulder. Extend your longe whip in front of him to stop his forward motion and to send him into the fence so that he turns in the other direction. As he makes the turn into the fence, snap your whip behind him to ask him to lope off in the new direction. Don't say "Whoa!"—that command is used *only* for a complete halt. Just extend your whip in front of him, send him in the other direction, and move him on. Ask him to roll back or turn a few times in either direction, then continue with your regular round-pen work.

If a two-year-old is clumsy at this maneuver, it may only indicate that he needs more time to mature and develop, or it may mean that he is not athletically inclined and therefore not a suitable candidate for reining work. Don't judge a horse *solely* on this maneuver, however. Don't push him or ask him to perform the rollback over and over again. Pushing a horse that is too young or physically underdeveloped can lead to physical and mental problems that are difficult, if not impossible, to overcome. He needs to be moving forward with some energy (and some speed) to do well at this maneuver.

Roll the horse back into the fence. He will pivot on his inside hind leg . . .

. . . and lift his front up and over his hocks, turn and go.

Look how close this horse's hocks are to the ground. Look at the power being generated. These are older horses that know the maneuver well!

TEACHING THIS MANEUVER WHILE MOUNTED IN THE ARENA

The first step in teaching this maneuver while mounted is to develop the cue for the horse to lift his shoulder further. While mounted, jog the horse about four feet along the inside of the fence. (The fence will be on the left in this example.) Signal your horse to stop by lightly lifting both reins and then releasing as he begins to come to a halt.

Lifting both reins raises the horse's shoulders so that he should stop with his hind legs underneath him. Don't say "Whoa!" As soon as he has almost stopped, so the momentum helps him to lift and roll, lift the left rein (nearest the fence) to turn the horse into the fence. Apply right (outside) leg pressure, to tell the horse to move away from leg pressure and turn into the fence. Then ride back in the opposite direction, bumping him forward if needed.

For example, as soon as his forward motion from the jog or trot has stopped, raise your left rein about six inches over the saddle horn to lift his left shoulder. Then, direct rein or turn him to the left into the fence. Use outside leg pressure at the girth to tell him to perform the rollback. Apply the neck-rein cue as well so that he also begins to associate it with turning while performing this maneuver. When you feel his front end lift up and his weight begin to rock back over his hocks, release the upward pressure on your left rein. Continue to ask him to turn into the fence using both the direct-rein cue and a right neck-rein cue. Be sure that you don't pull so hard on the neck rein that it tips the horse's nose in the opposite direction from that in which you wish to go.

Lift your rein closest to the fence to turn the horse into the fence.

Apply your neck rein and outside (left) leg . . .

. . . to turn the horse . . .

. . . and continue down the fence in the opposite direction.

Remember—the neck rein is only a signal or a cue. You *cannot* force a horse to turn more quickly by using the neck rein harder. At the same time, apply right-leg pressure to tell the horse to move away from pressure and go into the fence to the left. As the horse comes out of the turn and is moving straight forward down the fence, drop your hands back to a neutral position, and use both legs to send him forward.

You must create energy for the horse to stop correctly so that he can lift and turn. If a horse is lagging or is heavy on his front end, you will not get the lift-and-turn response. A responsive, light-on-his-feet horse will usually perform this exercise with less effort.

If the horse trots into the rollback, he should stop, roll back, and trot out. If he lopes into the rollback, he should stop, roll back, and lope off. Use your outside leg to ask for the rollback, then add pressure from both legs to cue either for a jog or lope. Your legs create the energy.

ASK AGAIN

Go down the fence twenty feet and ask the horse to stop. Turn back in the opposite direction and go down the fence again. To change directions, simply reverse the cues. Work on this maneuver for a few minutes, going back and forth, up and down the fence, and turning into the fence to change directions. Then go on to something else and come back to the rollback later in your training session. This is hard work for a horse, and you don't want to discourage him by making him perform it repeatedly. Training a reining horse takes a long time. A horse can only absorb so much from each lesson. Be prepared to put months of training into your horse, and do not get discouraged just because you do not see results instantly. Training takes time.

After a few weeks of performing this exercise, your horse will get lighter and lighter when you ask him to stop before changing directions. He is learning that he will be asked to stop and then turn. Therefore, he begins to prepare for the stop, lift and turn as he *feels* your weight or body change. He knows that a change of direction *may* be coming when you lift your rein hand, and he begins to pay attention to the slightest lift of your hand and shift of your weight. This is another way that you create lightness in a reining horse.

The horse's body may be bent somewhat into the turn in the initial stages of training, but the straighter he stays, the easier it will be later. By holding your neck rein somewhat snugly (against the outside of his neck) as you ask the horse to make the turn into the fence, you can control the amount of bend in his neck. This is similar to asking a horse to keep his body aligned from head to tail when you ask him to spin. A neck rein that is too loose allows him to bend his neck. A neck rein that is too tight can pull his nose in the opposite direction. Use just enough contact with his mouth to keep his head straight.

You must use your hands and legs independently to teach these maneuvers. Your body must stay upright and balanced. Don't interfere with the horse's way of going. It may feel somewhat awkward as you first attempt to do this, but it will become easier with time and practice. You may have to concentrate on which hand to lift or which leg to push. Try to plan ahead so that you don't mistakenly use the wrong hand or leg cue, thereby confusing the horse.

If you get no response when you start this rollback maneuver, you may need to increase your horse's energy level by escalating his speed slightly as you trot along the fence. It is the horse's impulsion moving into the rollback that creates the energy required to perform the maneuver well. A pleasure-type jog does *not* have enough impulsion.

The rollback is hard work for your horse. Be careful not to overdo it in a training session.

UNDERSTANDING THE ROLLBACK

As your horse begins to understand the rollback and performs it readily using the fence, ask him to perform the same maneuver without the fence. Trot forward in a straight line. Use your rein and weight aids to signal a stop. As the horse is coming to a stop, *with his weight still over his hocks,* use the energy created by that same forward motion to lift and turn with your inside rein and outside leg. Place the neck rein over the horse's neck to continue to prepare him for his future cue and to keep him as straight as possible. Apply your outside leg cue or bump him, if necessary, to send him out of the rollback at a trot. Later, when you ask your horse to lope, stop, and turn, he should then lope out of the rollback. Remember to cue consistently whether with or without the fence.

Spend a lot of time trotting and loping in straight lines. Trot straight forward, stop, roll back, and move off in the new direction. Practice this maneuver often. It will help your horse become more responsive to the bit and

will continue to teach him to elevate his shoulders and reach under with his hind legs. Reaching under with his hind legs will help with his sliding stops.

Ask him to trot, stop, roll back, and trot out. As he begins to have more impulsion going into the rollback, his hind legs will extend farther underneath him. A horse that moves slowly and lethargically will stop slowly and lethargically. You will get a better stop by making him move with more impulsion. I like to start a horse at a slower speed so that I can show him what I want. Then I increase the impulsion and eventually the speed after he has shown me that he understands. Going slower gives you more control and allows the horse time to digest and understand this new sequence of cues. Going faster, with more impulsion, will create a better rollback, but only after the horse understands what it is he is supposed to do. As his ability to roll back increases, his stop will get better.

Once your horse is mature physically, you can ask him to lope, stop, roll back, and lope out. The rollback teaches the horse to round his back as he extends his hind legs underneath him and elevates

A finished horse will plant his hind leg . . .

. . . and then lift his front end up and around and make the turn. Keeping your reins too tight, as shown here, raises your horse's head in the air and slows his departure. Give him the rein to go!

his shoulders. This puts his haunches closer to the ground in preparation for a truly spectacular sliding stop later.

Some horses will perform the rollback more readily on one side than on the other. Always check first for a physical problem if the horse seems off on one side. If your horse checks out okay physically, and you still find that he is not as responsive on one side as he is on the other, spend three-quarters of your riding time on that side until this evens out. Walk, jog, and lope in circles on the stiffer side. Correct the horse as needed to keep him upright and balanced.

Use your legs to increase or decrease the size of your circles (see Chapter 8). Ask your horse to move away from leg pressure whether going forward or backward. Continue to make him become more supple and balanced.

ANTICIPATING YOUR COMMANDS

If a horse begins to anticipate your commands, change what you had planned. If he anticipates a rollback to the left, ask him to stop and stand in place, or push him on and ask him to jog or lope forward another twenty feet; then roll back in the *opposite* direction.

Ask him to stop and then to walk forward ten feet. Another time, after he stops, drive him forward into the bridle, then release your cues to let him stop. Slowly pick up the slack in your reins and ask him to back up for six or eight steps. Then stop and let him relax.

Change the routine. Make him wait for and obey your commands. Don't let him outguess you. Don't let him learn that he can anticipate your cues and get rewarded for doing so. Be sure that you don't ask for the same maneuvers in the same place or in the same order. Vary your routine and keep your horse waiting and guessing.

Your goal throughout this rollback training is to have a horse that responds more readily to your cues. Teaching the rollback and continuing to use this exercise will also help with your sliding stops as your horse learns to put his hind legs more underneath himself. Teaching him to put his left hind leg underneath himself to roll back to the left, and then teaching him to put his right hind leg underneath himself when he rolls back to the right, will eventually help him put both hind legs underneath himself when he is asked to slide to a halt. While you may have to exaggerate these cues at first, the result will be a horse that responds to light aids that are barely seen.

Stopping in preparation for a rollback. Notice my stopping position.

He would be scored higher if he exited in the same tracks as he entered the rollback.

CHAPTER SEVENTEEN

Teaching Your Horse to Slide to a Stop

THE SLIDING STOP

The sliding stop is one of the most exciting moves that a reining horse makes. Picture a reining horse increasing his speed to a gallop as he runs down the length of the arena. When he is asked to stop, he rounds his back, almost as if he is sitting, to bring his hind feet underneath. He gets deep into the ground and stops as he paddles in a cadenced step in front. His shoulders remain elevated so that he can paddle, or continue to walk, with his front legs. As his momentum from the stop or slide decreases, he begins to come up out of the sitting position. If you ask him to perform his next maneuver just as he stops, *while his weight is still over his hocks,* he is perfectly set up to roll back or to back up. When a reining horse is asked to back up, he should flex at the poll and move backward in a straight line. If he is asked to roll back coming out of the sliding stop, he leaves one hind foot underneath himself to pivot up and over as he keeps his body straight.

An example of a good stop by Lynxs Peppy, a more finished horse.

TEACH WHOA!

To teach a horse to slide to a stop, you must first teach him on the ground that "Whoa!" means to stop and stand immediately. "Whoa!" is a command that should be taught to a horse from his earliest days with a halter and be enforced throughout his lifetime. It is *not* a command that a horse can question. "Whoa!" does not mean to slow down. "Whoa!" does not mean to stop in a few minutes. "Whoa!" means to stop *now* and to not move until given another command, whether from the ground or from his back.

You can teach a horse to obey the whoa command while leading or when he is on the longe line by using a chain under his nose one or two times. When you longe a horse, say the command once like you mean it. Then enforce your command with a quick tug and release. (*Never* pull steadily on a chain attached under a horse's nose. It can cause a horse to rear up and go over backwards because of the associated pain.) When the horse stops and stands still, walk up to him and praise him. Then ask him to go forward again. Repeat the tug or snap on the line with the verbal command

"Whoa!" until the horse learns to obey without an accompanying snap of the chain. When you ask him to halt and he obeys the verbal command alone, walk up to him and pat his neck to reward him. Give him a few minutes to relax and to understand that if he stops on the verbal command, he will not feel the snap of the chain under his nose. It is easiest to teach this by asking the first day in the round pen, but can be taught later with a little more work.

If anytime in a horse's career he will not stop from a verbal "Whoa!" either from the ground or from his back, go back to the longe line and *enforce* that he must stop. Never abuse the whoa command by saying it when you don't mean it. Say it once and give him a second to obey. Then say it again and tug and release on the line so that he understands that when you say "Whoa!" he better stop now.

BEGINNING TO RIDE

When you start riding a young horse, practice stopping from a walk with the verbal whoa command and a light lift of the reins—the signal to stop.

The sliding stop. (Cal's Pistol)

Slide tracks made by the above horse. Each horse has his own style of stopping!

The reins do not force a horse to stop—they are only a signal to tell him to stop. If you try to force a reining horse to stop by pulling on his mouth, he will stop on his front end and jam his front legs into the ground, bouncing to a halt. If your horse has been taught to obey the whoa command from the ground, after a few attempts he will probably stop from the verbal command followed by a light signal of the reins. Continue to ask verbally, and then enforce with the reins if needed. Whoa means whoa—stop right now!

Spend a lot of time jogging and then later loping in straight lines with your horse upright and between the bridle. As you continue teaching him to lift his shoulders and move in response to leg pressure, you will have the necessary tools to correct him if he does not travel in a straight line. If your horse leans or veers to one side (that is, if his body is not correctly aligned) use the corresponding leg and rein aid to correct him and make him travel straight forward. A horse's body must be aligned from head to tail in order for him to slide to a stop in correct form.

Your body must also be balanced evenly on either side of the horse. Think again of a child sitting on your shoulder, wiggling from side to side. Have you ever said to such a child, "Quit moving around before I drop you"? Your horse would probably love to be able to yell at you if you wiggle or sit off-balance as he tries to stop correctly. Your hips and shoulders should mirror one another, letting you sit exactly centered on the horse's back. Your rein hand should be centered directly above

PROTECTIVE BOOTS

I use splint boots on every horse I train, from day one until they retire. They're cheap insurance and can protect against leg injuries. I use skid boots when I begin to teach the stop so a horse doesn't stop so hard that he burns the hair off his fetlocks, which could make him hesitate to stop hard again.

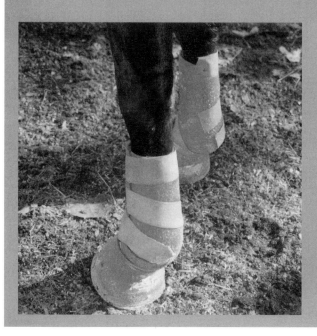 

Sit straight . . .

. . . not crooked—don't drop your shoulder or your hip.

the horse's mane. You should look straight ahead, focused on something at the far end of the arena, so that your body gives that straight-forward message to the horse.

You also must look ahead when you stop your horse, because that keeps your body evenly balanced over the horse. Your weight must be to the back of the saddle, not only as cue to tell the horse that you want to stop, but to help the horse put his weight back over his hocks. If you lean forward, not only could you go over his head and land on the ground, but you also weight the horse's front end. This makes it almost impossible for him to elevate his front and "sit" behind to stop correctly when you begin to add speed to this maneuver.

STOPPING AT THE JOG

Stopping a horse at the jog frees you from having to time your cues to ask for the stop at the right time. Later, when

you progress to stopping from a lope, you will have to ask at precisely the right sequence in his stride. Initially, when you ask a horse to stop from the jog, exaggerate your weight cue. Shift your weight back, say "Whoa!" and lightly lift the reins to signal a stop. Lift your reins lightly to signal the stop just as your weight drops to the back of the saddle. Think of sitting on your pockets.

Put your shoulders back, brace your lower back, and think of sitting on your pockets. Keep your seat firmly in the saddle and *slightly* brace your legs in front of you. Lift your reins so that the horse feels your signal to stop. Then release *when you feel him begin to stop*. When the horse has stopped, release all cues and sit relaxed, thereby telling him that he responded correctly. Give him time to absorb the cue, and the reward that followed, when he obeyed. If you rush your horse off to do something else, he might think that he has done something wrong and is being corrected. Sitting relaxed on his back after he stops will make him want to stop. This is especially helpful on a horse that tends to get "high" under pressure.

You cannot force a horse to stop. Too *harsh* a rein cue can cause a horse to fear the rein aid, making him "lock up" or bounce to a stop on his front legs. Although a horse can be taught to stop on a verbal or weight cue alone (as shown by the many horses that will stop bridleless in competition), teaching the rein cue can help. If your horse's attention wanders before you ask for a halt, using the reins can bring his attention back to the job at hand. But if you have never used the reins to signal a stop or taught the horse that the correct response to rein pressure is to flex at the poll and give to the bit, he might toss his head in the air and try to evade the rein signal. A horse must first learn to flex at the poll and to be soft in his mouth, which takes a lot of training time. A horse is not born knowing that a touch of the reins means to halt. Rely more on the verbal whoa command to halt. Most horses will stop correctly on their hind end from the verbal whoa, but *do* teach the rein cue as a backup message.

If you have a problem with a horse grabbing the bit and sticking his nose out when you ask him to stop (which sometimes happens when you go to the faster gaits), hold the reins just short enough so that he will bump his mouth when he sticks out his nose. There is a difference between a horse that grabs the bit and one that uses his head and neck to balance as he stops. Consider the horse's natural way of going before you apply a correction. Some horses naturally stop with their back rounded and their head low. This is a pretty sight, but not all horses can stop this way. Other horses must slightly raise their head and neck to balance.

Working on the other maneuvers, in addition to teaching the stop, will help your horse to slide. Rollback training will

The stopping position—heels down, sitting on your pockets.

teach him to round his back and extend his hind legs farther underneath himself, one side at a time. To roll back, the horse must elevate his shoulders—a very real requirement in the sliding stop—and reach underneath himself with his inside leg. As you work both left and right sides at the rollback, the horse learns to put both left and right legs underneath himself. Then, as you progress with the sliding stop, he will put both hind legs further underneath himself and his haunches will be lower to the ground, preparing him for a truly spectacular stop.

Continue to ask your horse to stop from a jog as you practice rollbacks. Then, as the horse learns to roll back by putting one hind leg deeper underneath himself, gradually begin asking for a stop from a trot, rather than from a jog. The trot, being faster, creates more impulsion. It is the impulsion going into the stop that allows the

Teach the rein cue to stop as a backup to your verbal "whoa!"

horse to get his hind legs underneath and prepares him for dazzling stops later. Because the horse has been taught to bring his left hind leg underneath himself to pivot over in response to the left rollback, and to bring his right hind leg underneath himself in response to the right rollback, his response to a light rein cue on both reins (used for the sliding stop) should bring both hind legs deeper underneath him. The reins create a barrier for his front end, and his hind legs slide up to meet this barrier. The impulsion and the deepness of the horse's hind legs, combined with elevated shoulders, allow a horse get into the ground and stop.

When you ask a horse to increase his speed, or gallop, going into the stop, he must reach further underneath himself with his hind legs to increase his speed. This causes him to run "uphill," elevating his shoulders and dropping his hindquarters, thus helping him to get into a position to slide. For now, practice by asking the horse to stop from a jog or trot. Then let him relax and enjoy the stop. Sit on his back quietly for a few minutes to teach him that a stop is a good thing—you ask him to stop and he gets to rest and relax. This teaches him not to run off after a stop. When you intersperse stops and rests with rollbacks or backups, your horse learns that he must wait for and obey your commands. This will keep him alert for your next cue.

Ask your horse to trot, stop, and roll back to the left a few times. Then ask him to trot, stop, and roll back to the right. Then ask him to stop and stand. Vary your routine. You do not want him to learn to anticipate your commands.

PROGRESS SLOWLY

Progress with your lessons slowly so as not to frighten the horse. He must learn to use his hind end, and he must develop those muscles. Don't push him past the point where he is physically or mentally ready. It takes at least a year to train a reining horse to be solid in these maneuvers. *Don't rush.*

Teach your horse to move forward and stop in a straight line. Especially during the beginning stages of training, never ask your horse to stop unless his body is straight and aligned from head to tail. Use your aids to correct him first before asking him to stop. If he stops and veers to the left, take your rein and make him turn twice as far to the right. Always make him turn in the opposite direction from the one that he chose.

Once your horse is stopping straight with his hind legs underneath him from a trot, you can begin to ask him to stop from a lope. Be sure that the footing is suitable for stopping. Before you ask a horse to stop from a lope, he should be shod with sliding plates.

Timing is crucial. You must ask at the right segment of his stride. When the horse has finished the loping stride—the downward segment of the lope—his front "leading" leg will be on the ground. That is the time to cue for the stop. The horse's hind legs will be up, allowing him to position them underneath, where they must be in order to stop.

Your rein hand must move slowly so that you don't grab the horse's mouth and scare him. Using the verbal whoa command will prepare the horse for a correct halt. Say "Whoa!" Lightly lift your hand, sit back in the saddle, brace your legs a bit forward, and let the horse stop. *As soon as the horse has begun to stop and you feel his body change underneath you, release the rein cue and let the horse slide to a stop on a loose rein. The reins are only a signal to tell him to stop.* Do not force him to stop by pulling harder, which will only frighten him and make him jam his front legs into the ground.

Sit back, sit deeply, and slightly brace your legs in front of you. If you are not prepared for the stop, you will feel as if you could go over his head. At the very least you will bump into the front of the saddle, and your changing body position will confuse the horse.

FENCING YOUR HORSE

Once your horse stops readily from the jog and he has been shod with sliding plates, you can begin "fencing" him. This will also help teach him to stop on a light cue. Loping your horse straight toward a fence set at the end of your sliding track will allow him to learn to stop without using the rein signal. It will also teach him to use his hind end better during the stop.

Keep a rein in each hand the first time or two so that he cannot run out to either side. Drive him straight toward the fence. Ten feet before you reach the fence, say "Whoa!" Use your body cues and let the fence actually stop the horse. When he stops, sit and let him relax. Again, vary your routine. You can roll back and lope off, you can ask the horse to back, or you can let him enjoy a brief rest for a job well done.

Fencing will help keep a horse honest. If you keep his head pointed directly toward the fence, he has no choice but to stop. Pulling on the reins is one reason why a horse stops with his head in the air. Fencing alleviates much of this problem, because the fence—not your reins—stops the horse.

Remember, a horse that stops from a slow lope does not have much impulsion going into the slide. He will drop his hind end and stop. However, you will not get the deep stops that you will get from a horse moving faster with more impulsion. Don't push for speed too soon, but when all is going well, go ahead and ask him to increase his speed

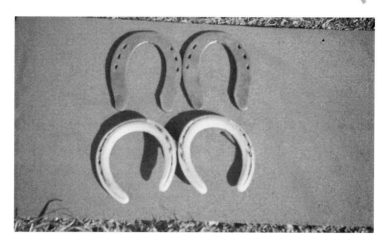

Reiners are shod on the hind feet with the sliding plates shown on the top and sometimes in front with the aluminum keg shoes shown on the bottom.

A horse shod with a sliding plate behind (the wide opening lets the dirt slide out) . . .

. . . and a keg shoe in front.

Trot or lope to a fence.

Say "Whoa."

on his way to a stop. Keep your rein cue light to stop him, and be sure that all of your cues are the same. Push your feet forward in the stirrups and get your weight back so that you can stay balanced as he stops. This will also prevent you from going over the horse's head and from hindering his way of stopping.

If you get a nice stop the first time, sit and reward your horse for a well-done maneuver so that he will try to repeat it. *Don't* push for more or ask him to stop hard over and over again. You may injure the horse or cause him to get resentful. Be sure that you have skid boots on your horse when you ask him to stop from a faster speed or you could burn the hair off his fetlocks. If this happens once or twice your horse will surely hesitate to stop hard the next time. Keep his comfort and willingness in mind so that he will have a long, sound, successful career.

TEACHING THE BACKUP

Teaching a horse to back up will also help with his sliding stops. Start by asking the horse to walk forward into the bridle by holding the reins and pushing him forward with your legs. This will collect or compress his body and will cause him to flex at the poll. When you stop squeezing your legs, the horse should stop. When he does stop, *immediately* release the rein pressure to let him know that he performed correctly. Then take the slack out of your reins by lifting your hand up slowly. Give the horse time to feel this new cue. With the rein barrier stopping his forward movement, cluck or use your legs to ask for motion. Because of the rein barrier, the only place left for the horse to go is backward.

When he backs up one step, release all pressure and praise him. Ask for one step the first day and two the second, and then gradually increase the number. Because the reins move as you lift them to ask him to back, your horse soon will learn that when he feels the slack coming out of the reins, he should flex at the poll, give to the bit, and begin to back up. Hold your rein tension steady at the point where he begins to back and let him keep backing up with your reins in that position. Release the reins *forward* to stop him.

As your horse backs, you can correct any deviation from a straight backward line with your legs. Your hands signal to the horse that he must back up, and your legs tell—or correct—the direction in which the horse is moving. A horse will move away from leg pressure going both forward and backward. Practice making the horse move his hip to the right by using your left leg, or to the left by using your right leg. Practice until you know how much of a cue it takes to make him respond and where it is best applied to get the desired result. Remember to use your cues consistently. *Ask for the same response from each cue placed in the same spot.* A horse knows the difference between a leg-pressure cue placed at the girth, which tells him to move his entire body sideways, and one placed two inches behind the girth, which tells him to move only his hip.

Don't ask for many backward steps or for a lot of speed yet. Correctness and softness are the important elements to teach now. Speed will come later. If the horse veers to either side, use your legs to push his hind end in the appropriate direction. As he learns to back up

If a horse gives you a hard time about backing or doesn't seem to understand, use a gate to force him to back. Pull it towards him as you cue with the reins.

correctly and consistently, cluck slightly ahead of his current rhythm to ask for an increase in his backward speed.

CONDITION FIRST

Your young horse must first mature both mentally and physically. His body must be physically ready to work. As with any athlete, this is accomplished

In time, a horse should flex at the poll, and back willingly.

Teach him to back straight by backing down the fence.

through conditioning. Don't expect to pull your horse out of the pasture once a week and have him ready to perform these demanding maneuvers.

Work on taking any resistance out of the horse as you begin to condition him. You will be that much further along when he is fit and ready to start working on the reining maneuvers. Show him that it is easier to obey than to disobey. Use your aids consistently. If you don't confuse your horse by changing how you ask for a specific maneuver, he should progress a little each day.

EVALUATING YOUR REINER

Conformation determines what a horse can do, as does his mind, his willingness to perform, and his athletic ability. Some horses can perform the other reining maneuvers, but cannot slide to a stop. It may be that their rump is too high or that their hind legs are not underneath their body.

A horse's mind is also important. A pretty horse that does not want to perform will never do as well as a horse that wants to do as you ask, no matter what he looks like. A good-looking horse is part of the whole picture, yet a solid, consistent horse will always score higher than a pretty, inconsistent horse. A "hot" horse (one that is anxious to be on the move at all times) probably cannot take the pressure when you get to a show. He may do reasonably well at home, yet blow up at a show. Horses that stay high after being asked to perform a maneuver with speed at home are sure to be that way at a show.

If you start having problems, it may be time to reevaluate your reining prospect. Training can only overcome so much. A quiet horse can usually be taught to gallop and to turn around with a degree of speed, but it is sometimes difficult to teach a "hot" horse to slow down and relax. However, as with anything, there is always the exception to the rule.

The training your horse has received so far will make him a better pleasure horse, trail horse, working ranch horse, or all-around family mount. Just because he may not have what it takes to compete as a reiner does not mean that you have wasted your training time. Simply put, this is the time to evaluate where your horse's real potential lies and plan the remainder of his training to take full advantage of that potential.

Stopping—both hind legs go under the belly as he paddles in front.

CHAPTER EIGHTEEN

Using and Refining the Aids

NATURAL AND ARTIFICIAL AIDS

Aids are tools that tell a horse what to do. Hands, seat, weight, and leg aids are natural, while running martingales, spurs, and draw reins are artificial. While it is best to rely on natural aids to encourage a horse, sometimes artificial aids must be used to further "convince" a horse of your objectives. Natural aids may be used independently, such as a single leg aid, or in combination, such as a hand and leg aid given at the same time. Natural aids may also be used in combination with artificial aids; for example, using your spur to enforce your leg cue, or using draw reins to encourage a horse to drop his head as you push him up into the bridle.

Before a horse can execute the proper response to any given aid, he must have time to feel, analyze, and react to the aid. More important, if a horse is to understand a cue, it must be given in a clear, concise, and consistent manner. A horse cannot obey an aid that he does not understand.

Artificial aids.

Spurs can help to make a horse more responsive. Some horses need them, some don't.

ACTIVE AND INACTIVE AIDS

Aids are either active or inactive, depending on your desired response, your request, or the horse's response at a given time. An active aid signals the horse what to do, as when you use a left-leg cue to tell the horse to lope on the right lead. In the simplest sense, your right leg is inactive or off the horse's side. Your inactive aids—hands, legs, or weight—should always be ready to assist the active aids.

When asking a horse to depart from a walk into a lope on the left lead, your reins first become active. You take a light hold of the horse's mouth to signal to him that a change is coming. Next, you push your horse up into the bridle with a light squeeze from both legs to prepare him to lope. Then your left leg becomes inactive or off his side, and your right leg becomes active to tell him to lope. As he steps into the lope, your reins now become inactive as you release his head to let him lope.

Once your horse responds, your right leg also becomes inactive as you stop applying the cue to lope. As long as he is loping correctly, you should sit quietly and let him lope. Only when he needs to be told to change what he is doing or to fix something that he is doing wrong should you apply another aid. If your horse throws his hip to the outside of the circle, your right leg would again become active. Applied behind the girth, it would tell the horse to keep his hip in the correct arc of the circle. If he begins to drift to the left or to the center of the pen, your left leg at the girth would hold or push him out to the rail.

If a horse is to understand a cue, it must be given in a clear, concise, and consistent manner.

The Reins

If you think that the reins are the most important aid, remember that they are only a way to *signal* to the horse to halt or to turn. If you think about it, thin strips of leather attached to a horse's

Thin strips of leather would not stop this horse if he didn't want to be stopped.

mouth cannot physically stop a 1,000-pound animal racing along at thirty miles per hour. The reason a horse obeys those thin strips of leather is because he has been taught that if he stops, the pressure on his mouth will be released. However, if the cue or the pressure on the reins is not released when the horse does obey and stop, why should he stop the next time? Why should he obey your rein signal? What is his reward for stopping? You must think about what you are telling your horse with *each and every move that you make*. Be careful not to abuse an aid if you expect your horse to respond to light aids.

Your Weight

Horses learn weight aids easily if you are consistent. If every time that you ask your horse to halt from a lope you sit more upright, bringing your shoulders back and bracing your lower back slightly, and stop following the motion of the horse with your body, he will learn this as a signal to halt. Reining horses do not perform the long, gliding stops that you see because the *reins* force them to slide—quite the opposite. If a horse is forced to stop through a harsh rein cue, he will jam his front end into the ground and bounce to a stop on his forehand.

A reining horse is taught to obey a light *signal* to halt. Through months of training, he learns that the rider's weight and a light touch of the reins are the cues to slide to a stop. He is taught to drop his hind end closer to the ground, to elevate his shoulders so that he can paddle in front, and to slide to a graceful halt. He does this with no resistance, not the way he would if you grabbed his mouth. No force is applied. The horse slides to a stop because he has been *taught* to halt in that manner. He respects the light rein and weight cues as the signal to halt, rather than being forced to halt by a strong pull on the reins.

Horses learn to stop by the shift of your weight.

Your Legs

Your legs are a way to signal the horse to go forward, but they do not *make* him go forward. Your legs cannot make a horse go forward when you are sitting on his back. A horse must be taught to obey your leg cue. You teach him to obey a light leg cue by enforcing the original light asking cue. You first lightly *ask* him to go forward at your chosen gait. If he does not obey, you *tell* him to go forward using a somewhat stronger cue. Then, if you must, you *insist* that he go forward by using an even stronger cue, such as a tap from the crop (or spurs if you have a secure lower leg). By using this sequence of asking, telling, and enforcing, you teach your horse that it is to his benefit to obey the original light asking aid. You reward the horse by releasing the pressure of your go-forward cues as soon as he begins to respond. This teaches him that the sooner he obeys, the lighter your request will be.

Your legs can help to control the direction of a horse. If a horse wobbles

To cue for a spin to the right, the rider is pressing with the left (active) leg and opening the right (inactive) leg.

learns that you want him to *move away* from pressure.

REFINING THE AIDS

Feel What Your Horse Is Doing

You must feel what your horse is doing and then apply the hand, leg, or weight aid that will best tell him what to do. If your horse veers to the inside of a circle, use your inside leg to push him out. If he drops a shoulder and falls into the circle, use your inside rein to lift his inside shoulder. If he tries to slow down, use both legs to send him forward. Most importantly, if the horse is performing correctly, sit quietly and leave him alone as a reward. The aids are only to be used when you must tell the horse what to do or when to make a change.

Use Each Aid Independently

You must have the ability to use each aid independently of the rest of your body and of the other aids. For example, if your horse is veering to the inside of a left-hand circle, you must be able to push *only* your left leg to his side to send him back out. You must learn to use your legs independently of one another to send the horse over and out while your hands allow the horse freedom of his head and neck. If you have not yet learned to balance or to ride without squeezing your legs to stay on, you may inadvertently cue your horse without realizing it. It is unfair to punish a horse when you are cueing him with your legs by bumping his sides and using your legs to balance. If your horse is not responding correctly to what you

side to side, rather than going straight forward (as sometimes happens when a horse sees a scary obstacle), use both legs to send him straight forward. Think of squeezing his energy out the front. Using both legs sends him forward as you block the door for him to move diagonally left with your active right leg, and vice versa.

Leg cues not only tell the horse to go forward, they can tell a horse to spin, to move laterally or two-track, to roll back, or to take a certain lead. An untrained horse will push into pressure, not move away from it. Through months of training, he

Any time your horse is performing correctly, sit quietly and leave him alone as a reward.

think you are asking, find an instructor or experienced rider to help you determine if you are cuing your horse inadvertently.

Form a Partnership

Form a partnership with your horse. Your guidelines should state, "If I use this cue and you react as I have taught you, I will release all aids and sit quietly. Only when I need to tell you to perform a transition will I again apply an aid to tell you what to do next. I promise not to continue to apply the aids when you are performing correctly. I will give you time to think, react, and then perform before I correct you. However, if you do not do as I ask, I will apply progressively stronger aids to enforce my command until you do as I ask."

As your skills develop, you will *feel* whether your horse is moving correctly and therefore should be left alone, or if he is moving incorrectly and should be corrected. You will begin to interpret what you feel, rather than having to look or guess, and you will know instinctively which aid to use to correct him. You will have the tools (aids) to correct a horse's response, sometimes even *before* he takes a wrong step. With the proper use of the aids, you will be able to influence how a horse reacts initially. As your horse progresses in training, the slightest shift of your weight or the lightest touch of a rein or leg will tell your horse exactly what you want him to do.

Learning how, when, and why to use each available aid takes time, patience, and practice. Days, months, even years can fly by before you feel that you know them well. And just when you do, along comes a new horse to teach you new things.

Reward your horse for good behavior by sitting quietly on her and allowing her to relax.

CHAPTER NINETEEN

Correcting Bad Habits

LOOK FOR THE CAUSE

It often seems that bad behavior is easier to establish in a horse than good behavior. There are a couple of reasons. First, a horse will act in a way that is more comfortable for him, and second, he may feel that he has accomplished what he wanted to do rather than what you wanted to do. In the first example, many horses are lazy and would rather not exert themselves. They choose to perform a maneuver so that it is easiest for them. It's also possible that you are pushing the horse past what he is capable of giving at that point in time, thus causing him to become frustrated. He may toss his head, stop, stand in place and refuse to move, or even begin to rear. These are signals that you need to back up a step and prepare your horse more slowly for the new maneuver before you ask again.

If a horse begins to resent a maneuver that he has performed well in the past, check for a physical problem. Has he lost a shoe? Does he have a stone bruise? Is he muscle sore? Does he have sharp edges or wolf teeth that need to be filed or removed? Check for physical reasons first, because asking a horse to work when something is hurting him is not fair.

If the horse checks out physically, look for a mental reason. Have you drilled and drilled on a maneuver until the horse is bored with it? Horses need some variety and the occasional easy day to stay fresh in mind. They can have an off day, just as you do. Sometimes it is best to ask again tomorrow for that maneuver and see if the horse behaves better. Perhaps you did not "explain" exactly what it was that you wanted him to do. Your horse can get frustrated or confused, just as you would, with unclear directions. He may react badly, almost in self-defense. Some horses will choose to test you now and then. These horses need the occasional reminder of who is boss in the relationship. Other horses will misbehave to get you off their back sooner so that they can go back to the stall or pasture to eat or rest.

A horse that is trying to rush through a lesson to return to the barn can be helped by leaving him fully tacked with the saddle tightened and tying him in his stall or to a tree or post outside.

As always, when behavior problems arise, check for a physical cause.

155

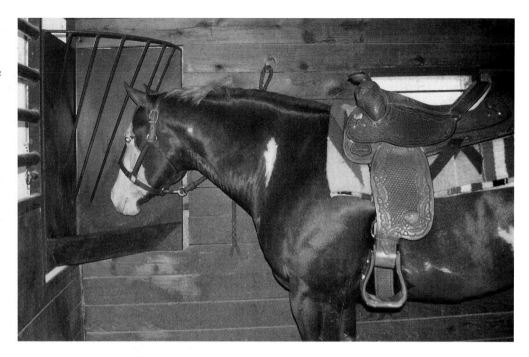

Leave him tied for thirty minutes to an hour. Do this every day after you ride and see if it helps his behavior. Be sure to end the lesson on a good note so that the horse learns the lesson doesn't end until he behaves.

FIX IT SOONER

As with most equine training problems, the sooner a horse is corrected for misbehavior, the easier it is to fix and the less likely it will become a habit. A horse can learn a habit after as few as three repetitions of a given behavior. Correcting a horse the first time that he misbehaves is best. If, for example, your horse stops at the gate and refuses to go forward and you dismount, you are *rewarding* him for misbehaving. You must think about what each and every action on your part is telling the horse. Learn to think like a horse and try to determine how he may interpret your cues or actions.

If your horse refuses to take a certain lead and you stop him and sit on his back in frustration, you are rewarding the horse. You are telling him that he has behaved correctly. What is his in-

centive for taking the correct lead when he gets rewarded for taking an incorrect lead? Why should he take a correct lead and have to work when you let him rest when he is "bad"?

If your horse bucks every time that you ask him to lope and you do not show or tell him that bucking is unacceptable, he will continue to buck to show his displeasure at being made to work. However, be very sure that you have not popped the horse in the mouth with the bit every time you asked him to lope. In that instance the horse might be bucking in self-defense. He knows that loping those first few strides will cause him to get jerked in the mouth and he wants to to avoid the pain in his mouth. Watch your equitation.

CORRECT EVERY TIME

Correcting a horse every time he makes a mistake will show him that it is to his advantage to obey your original cue. The correction that I use most often is pulling a horse into two or three tight little circles, always in the opposite direction of that which the horse has chosen. For example, if the horse tries to run out the gate to the left, I pull him into three small circles to right. If he cuts into the center of the ring to the right, I pull him to the outside of the ring or to the left. If the horse begins to buck, I pull him in three tight little circles in either direction.

This is not an extremely harsh correction. I see no sense in spurring or in beating a horse with a whip. Either of those corrections will generally make the horse bolt forward, and then you have to pull on his mouth to make him stop. You have just taught the horse to bolt, which is unacceptable, and you have pulled on his mouth, making it tougher.

The only time I will strike a horse with a crop or bat is when he tries to bite or kick. In this case you are justified in making a severe correction because your safety is at stake. Don't play around—let the horse know that this type of behavior is totally unacceptable under any circumstances and that he will be corrected severely (within reason, of course).

Correcting a horse by using small circles can be increased in severity if you take your outside leg and bump him hard with your heel as he is circling. Yelling in a low tone of voice or "growling" at him will also help to show your displeasure. Horses learn quickly that a soothing "good boy" means that they are performing correctly and that a sharp "quit" or other verbal correction means that they are not. Once a horse learns these verbal cues, you can sometimes use them alone without an accompanying physical correction. You will have to read your horse to see if a verbal cue is effective or if he needs a stronger correction. I always try the lightest correction first and work my way up from there.

Don't dismount by the gate. Stop in the center every time!

Don't reward your horse by the gate. He'll try to stop every time he goes by the gate to get his rest or reward.

GIVE HIM TIME TO UNDERSTAND

In order for a horse to understand a correction, a horse must be corrected every time he performs a bad behavior. After enough corrections, he will eventually think that the crime is not worth the punishment and that it is to his benefit to obey the original request. You must be consistent and follow through with your corrections no matter how long it takes, if you expect your horse to understand. Horses do not learn or unlearn a behavior in a day. Training takes time.

One of the biggest advantages in sending a horse to a trainer is that the trainer will ride your horse daily—day after day after day. You do not have to find the time to ride after work, after the kids are in school, or after the housework is done. Riding is a trainer's job, often involving six days a week, eight to twelve hours a day. A trainer must find the time to do other chores after the horses are ridden. A horse with a trainer will learn, or unlearn a bad behavior, more quickly because he is consistently ridden five or six days a week.

Don't get discouraged if your horse does not learn or unlearn a behavior in one lesson or one day. Training a horse takes a large commitment of time, a large dose of patience, and much perseverance. I see many students that are ready to give up on a horse, when in fact they have just begun.

If you correct your horse only every second or third time he misbehaves, he will try again and again to misbehave. He will wonder, "Is today a day I get corrected? Or is it a day that I can get away with it?" Don't confuse a horse by letting him act a certain way one day, then correcting him for that same behavior the next day. *Consistency is the key to good training*, no matter how monotonous it may become to you.

TIME YOUR CORRECTIONS

Timing is also extremely important. If you want your horse to understand a

You only have three seconds in which to give an effective correction. Otherwise, the horse won't understand what the correction was for.

correction, you must give it within three seconds of the misbehavior. Otherwise, too much time has passed and the horse will think that you are correcting him for something totally unrelated. Correcting a horse as soon as he begins a bad behavior is the *only way* that he will understand. Using the example of a horse that tries to cut into the center of the arena, or to cut a circle short to head toward the gate, you must, *as soon as* the horse heads in that direction, take hold of the reins (gently—no snatching or jerking on the reins) and pull him into tight circles in the opposite direction. A horse does not like this. It is uncomfortable for him to bend in a tight, small circle.

When you begin to pull a horse into small circles, you must be sure to loosen the outside rein so that he has room to turn his head in the pulling direction. If your horse is strong, hold or lock your pulling hand on your hip. This gives you a little extra power that can keep the horse from pulling the rein out of your hand or from pulling your hand forward, in effect, rewarding himself by release of pressure.

If you know that your horse may try to misbehave in a certain section of the arena and that you might have to correct him, be prepared. Think ahead, and be prepared. Training is all about outthinking a horse.

ASK AGAIN AND AGAIN

Correct the horse and then *ask the horse to perform that same maneuver again.* Allow him to *begin* to make the mistake. Correct him again, and then repeat this sequence. After a few series of corrections, you should begin to see results, although with some horses it may take a few days or even a few weeks or months. This will depend upon the nature of the problem, the length of time the horse has been acting this way, and your own perseverance and consistency.

DON'T WAIT

You cannot wait two or three minutes to see if the horse will behave on his own. Every time you do that, the horse thinks that it is acceptable to act in the way he chooses. Repeating the correction consistently, within three seconds, will communicate to your horse that he will get corrected every time he begins to make that mistake. Be fair to him by being consistent. Let him learn the rules.

TRAIN TO FIT THE HORSE

Horses have different personalities, temperaments, and levels of ease or difficulty in training. Some horses give in easily, while others need to be "convinced"

Reward your horse for good behavior—not bad.

that it is in their best interest to obey. Some horses seem to learn almost on their own. You must consider your horse's personality and plan your training program around that. Don't push for too much, too soon. Long, slow, and steady will give more lasting results. At the same time, don't let a horse start a bad behavior that you will have to fix tomorrow.

Adjust your training schedule to fit *your* horse. Is he quiet? You may need to plan some long gallops to keep him interested. A quiet horse can become bored with the same slow, daily work and may start bad habits out of boredom. Change his mind from time to time by galloping in large circles or doing transitions. Is your horse "hot"? A lot of slow, steady work will let him learn that no unexpected challenges are right around the corner. Let him stay in a given gait until he settles. Spend time walking quietly, spinning slowly (once you get to that point), stopping, and letting him stand and relax with you on his back. Let him know that you will not put him in a situation that will hurt him. Corrections for this type of horse often need to be lighter than with

a quieter horse. You don't want a "hot" horse to get excited so that he blows up. You must stay relaxed. Your body language—calm, quiet and relaxed—tells the horse that all is well.

Starting with a young horse and correcting each problem before it becomes a habit is the ideal. However, life is seldom ideal. You will have to work with whatever problems your horse may have previously acquired, and also teach the new maneuvers that you wish him to learn. Training takes time and patience. "Talk" to your horse in a language that he can understand, and reward him when he performs well or to the best of his ability at that point in his training. Correct him when he is wrong and show him how he should have performed. Break each lesson down to its simplest component and build on that. Given enough time, with consistent, fair training methods, most horses are able to learn new behaviors. Remember, however, to take a horse's conformation into account. Some horses are physically unable to perform certain maneuvers, or at least as to perform them as well as a more correctly built horse.

Watch your horse as he moves freely through the pasture and think of how you can tell him to act that way under saddle.

CHAPTER TWENTY

How Reining Horses Are Scored

THE NRHA SCORING SYSTEM

The scoring system used by the National Reining Horse Association was developed in 1984 by John Snoblen, then an NRHA board member, with the help of Dick Pieper, president of the association at the time. This popular form of evaluation has now been adopted by many other equine associations for reining competition.

Start with a Seventy

Every reiner enters the ring with a score of seventy, which is considered average. From that score, points are either added or subtracted for the quality of the maneuvers, and penalties are assessed for violations. Each reining pattern has either seven or eight maneuver groups, scored individually, with the total points tallied to give the final score.

Add and Subtract

The NRHA judging rules state that an excellent maneuver receives a plus one and one-half; a very good maneuver, a plus one; a good maneuver, a plus one-half. A correct maneuver receives a zero. Using this system, if your horse

performs the entire pattern correctly but without appreciable smoothness, finesse, positive attitude, or controlled speed, he receives a seventy (no plus or minus points for any maneuver).

A horse that loses form receives a minus one-half for a poor maneuver, a minus one for a very poor maneuver, and a minus one and one-half for an extremely poor maneuver. In some cases, a horse may gain or lose on a similar maneuver within a pattern. For example, he could mark a plus one for his first stop and a minus one on his second. Using this system, the final score reflects the total of the entire pattern.

Besides a numerical score (like a seventy or a seventy and one-half) for the entire pattern, it is possible to receive a score of zero or a "no score."

A Score of Zero

A score of zero for the entire pattern results from various violations, such as the use of more than the index or first finger between the reins, the use of two hands, failure to complete the pattern as outlined, or adding maneuvers not specified. Balking or refusal to perform, running away, overspinning or underspinning by more than one-quarter turn, or a fall by

Drop the bridle to show the judge the bit at the end of every run.

either horse or rider also results in a score of zero.

A No Score

A no score is assessed when a contestant abuses an animal, shows disrespect or misconduct, or uses illegal equipment. All bits must be free of mechanical devices and have rounded, smooth mouthpieces, the diameter being no less than five-sixteenths of an inch. Curb chains at least one-half inch in width are acceptable as long as they are free of barbs or twists. After each run, the bit must be dropped to show the judge the equipment.

Don't confuse a score of zero (for the pattern) with a score of zero for a maneuver. They are definitely different. A maneuver score is what you receive for an individual maneuver and is a measure of how well you perform it. If you receive zeros on all maneuvers in a pattern, your run will score a seventy, which is average. A score of zero for the entire run means that you or your horse did something wrong (as in a violation) and your entire pattern receives a zero. In that case, you will not place at all.

THE KEY TO SCORING WELL

The key to scoring well on any pattern is correctness. A horse performing the pattern exactly as it is written will score higher than one that runs a sloppy pattern.

When asking a horse to spin, use the first one-quarter of your spin to set the horse in the correct motion. Then build speed. As you approach the last one-quarter of your last spin, be prepared to ask your horse to "shut down," or stop spinning, at the exact point called for by the pattern.

In patterns that call for lead changes at the center of the pen, the center can be described as an area approximately ten feet to either side of the absolute middle. Choose ground that will allow your horse to perform to the best of his ability. If you ask for a sliding stop on sticky ground, the horse might not be able to do it.

Increasing speed going into a stop on good ground will actually allow your reiner to stop better. Because he must reach underneath himself with his hind legs to build speed, he elevates his front end, in effect running uphill. This allows him to lock his hind legs underneath his body as his shoulders are elevated. He can then get into the ground to stop.

When a pattern calls for a hesitation, hesitate for a few seconds, and then go on to the next maneuver. Obviously, a horse that moves nervously in place will score lower than a horse that waits quietly for his next command.

In each pattern, you are required to back up at least ten feet. In the patterns that require you to run down the middle and stop, then back up to the center of

A quiet horse will score higher than an excited, nervous one.

the arena, always plan your stop so that you can back up at least ten feet before stopping at the center of the pen. If your horse is a fancy backer, go farther past center to show off his talent. However, if backing is not one of your horse's highlights, back up only the required distance. Know your horse's strong points and show them off. Minimize the distance or the speed on his weak points.

USE CORRECT FORM

A horse that performs the entire pattern with correct form but with moderate speed should always score higher than a horse that performs with speed but loses form. For example, asking a horse to spin faster than his training allows usually causes him to lose form. The horse might hop or bounce, rather than stay flat, or he will be unable to keep his inside hind pivot foot locked in place. (In reality, the pivot foot constantly adjusts,

but it appears to stay in place.)

PENALTIES

Staying out of the penalty box is one of the surest ways to place in a reining, and more reinings have been won in that manner than any other. Penalties are assessed for maneuver infractions.

RULE BOOKS AND PLANNING

Contact the NRHA to get a current rule book and study it carefully. It is important that you stay abreast of any changes. Walk through the pattern in your mind before you enter the ring. Memorize the pattern and plan for any idiosyncracies your horse may have. Do your best and remember that even the best of trainers have gone off-course on a pattern at some point in their career.

PENALTIES

There are various ways to incur penalties. Here are some of them and how to avoid them.

- STARTING YOUR CIRCLES OR FIGURE-EIGHTS ON THE WRONG LEAD, AS WELL AS A DELAYED CHANGE OF LEAD. These are penalized as follows:
    Delayed change of lead for one stride, penalized one-half point; from start to one-quarter of the circumference of a circle, penalized one point; from start to one-half of the circumference of a circle, penalized two points; from start to three-quarters of the circumference of the circle, penalized three points. A complete circle in the wrong lead is penalized four points.

- IF YOU TROT UP TO TWO STRIDES WHEN STARTING A CIRCLE OR COMING OUT OF A ROLL-BACK, YOU ARE PENALIZED ONE-HALF POINT. TROTTING FOR MORE THAN TWO STRIDES, BUT FOR LESS THAN A HALF-CIRCLE OR HALF THE LENGTH OF THE ARENA, IS PENALIZED TWO POINTS.

- A BREAK OF GAIT IN THE PATTERN IS PENALIZED BY TWO POINTS.

- FREEZING UP IN SPINS OR ROLLBACKS IS PENALIZED BY TWO POINTS.

- WHEN A RIDER SPURS A HORSE IN FRONT OF THE CINCH, HOLDS THE SADDLE WITH EITHER HAND, OR USES THE FREE HAND TO PRAISE OR INSTILL FEAR, A FIVE-POINT PENALTY IS ASSESSED.

- IF THE HORSE INDULGES IN BLATANT DISOBEDIENCE, SUCH AS KICKING, BITING, OR REARING, THERE IS A FIVE-POINT PENALTY.

- OVERSPINNING OR UNDERSPINNING BY ONE-EIGHTH OF A TURN IS A ONE-HALF POINT PENALTY; BY MORE THAN ONE-QUARTER TURN, YOU RECEIVE A SCORE OF ZERO FOR THE ENTIRE PATTERN. BE SURE TO COUNT YOUR SPINS CORRECTLY.

- IN PATTERNS THAT REQUIRE A HORSE TO RUN AROUND THE END OF THE ARENA, THE HORSE MUST REMAIN A MINIMUM OF TWENTY FEET FROM THE WALL OR FENCE WHEN APPROACHING A STOP OR ROLLBACK. IF YOU DO NOT, YOU'LL BE PENALIZED ONE-HALF POINT. PLUS, IF YOUR HORSE IS TOO CLOSE TO THE WALL, HE WILL NOT HAVE ENOUGH ROOM TO ROLL BACK CORRECTLY. ALSO, ROLLBACKS MUST BE MADE TOWARD THE CLOSEST WALL ON RUNAROUNDS.

Enter the ring planning to do your best on that day with your horse. If he is not capable of running with blazing speed at home, do *not* expect him to run a blazing pattern at a show. Ask for as much you know your horse can give. Show him to the best of his ability at that point in his training. Pushing for more not only runs the risk of losing form; it can also sour or scare the horse and set his training back days or weeks. Correct form is always scored higher than speed with incorrect form. Remember—there is always another show.

WALK THROUGH A RUN

Now we will talk your way through a run using NRHA pattern number six:

Your horse, Calooa, walks into the arena on a loose rein, ears perked and showing a pleasant expression. He stops and hesitates at the exact center of the pen and waits for your command. When asked to make four spins to the right, he steps slowly into the spin and builds speed as he turns around. By the end of the first turnaround, he is at full speed with his body flat. He stops at the exact spot where he started, facing the same wall.
Score: Plus 1

He hesitates a second. Although it is not required, it shows his willingness to wait for the next cue. He steps into a left spin and again builds speed as he turns. By the last turnaround, he is at full speed, but you cue him a bit late. When asked to stop, he overspins by one-quarter turn.
Score: Minus 1/2

You cue him with an outside leg and Calooa departs into a left-lead lope. By the halfway point of this circle, he is galloping. He gallops in two large, fast circles. As he approaches the center of the

pen, you sit up and Calooa slows to a pleasure-horse lope to complete a small, slow circle. At the center of the pen, he changes leads, although he jumps when he feels your cue asking for the change.
Score: Minus 1

By the first half of the new circle, he is galloping at a good speed. He gallops in two large, fast circles. At the center point of the arena, you sit up, and again, on a barely seen cue, Calooa slows to a pleasure-horse lope. He completes a small, slow circle with his body bent into the correct arc of the circle. He changes leads easily in the center of the pen.
Score: Plus 1

After he crosses the center of the pen, he begins a large, fast circle to the left. He does not close this circle but runs up the right side of the arena past the center marker and is only ten feet from the wall. He slides to a stop (the stop is not required, but it gives you a chance to show your horse if he is a fancy stopper—and he does have to stop to roll back). He performs a right rollback toward the wall without hesitating. A noise in the bleachers attracts his attention and he jogs for two steps before loping.
Score: Minus 1

He begins to run back around the previous circle but does not close this circle. He runs past the center marker, slides to a stop, and performs an average left rollback.
Score: 0

He lopes off nicely and increases his speed to a gallop as he runs around the previous circle. He gallops up the right side of the arena past the center marker and does a sliding stop, this time twenty feet from the wall. He locks his hind legs underneath his belly and slides for thirty feet, dragging his tail behind him.

He stands up out of the slide, yet keeps his weight over his hocks as he waits for his next command. He flexes at the poll and backs up twenty feet in a straight line.

Score: Plus 1 1/2

Calooa stops and hesitates to show that the pattern is completed. You guide Calooa toward the judge on a loose rein to show that he is easily controlled and not excited over the previous run. You dismount and remove the bridle so that the judge may inspect the bit.

Calooa receives a score of seventy-one. This is a good score and one that could place at many of the local shows. Many variations of this type of score happen time after time. Occasionally, luck plays a part in it, as it did in this horse's score. His attention wandered just long enough for him to lose points. Rider error often plays a part in a horse's score as it did here by the horse cuing late in the spin and hooking him with a spur when asking for a lead change. However, this horse shows potential. He spins flat, has long, gliding stops, and shows no signs of resentment. His future scores may increase. But even if they do not, he is a pleasure to ride and will bring many hours of enjoyment. And that is what reining is all about.

Always read your current rule book to stay abreast of new changes.

APPENDIX

Fourteen Tips for Successful Training

Remember, the desired end of your training program is to have a horse that responds to light, barely visible aids with you moving as little as possible to tell the horse what you want.

1. RESPECT

Respect starts on the ground and carries over to work under saddle. If a horse does not respect a whoa command given from the ground, why should he respect or obey it when given from his back?

> *Example:* The first step in teaching a reiner to slide to a stop is to teach him— on the ground—that "Whoa!" means to stop immediately.

2. FEEL

You must be able to feel when a horse is right and therefore should be left alone, and when he is wrong and therefore should be corrected.

> *Example:* You feel a horse make a mistake, for example, pick up a wrong lead, drop a shoulder, or drift away from the rail. You can correct it immediately without having to look or guess if the horse is right or wrong. Or you feel the horse depart on the correct lead and you sit quietly and let him lope.

3. TIMING

Your corrections and rewards must occur immediately at the start of the bad or good behavior. If you wait longer than three seconds to punish or reward, the horse will not understand why he is being corrected or rewarded.

> *Example: Correction:* If you let a horse lope twice around the arena to the right on the left lead, before pulling him back to a walk to ask him again for a correct right-lead lope, he will not understand that you are correcting him for taking the incorrect left lead.
> *Reward:* Your horse correctly departs in a controlled right lead lope. Sit quietly and let him lope.

4. RIDING ABILITY

As a rider or trainer, you must have the ability to know exactly what your hands and legs or weight cues are telling the horse at all times. If you use your cues accidentally, without meaning to or in an inconsistent manner, your horse will not be able to decipher which cue is meant to tell him something that he must respond to and which cue he can ignore because you "did not mean it." Every time you ride, you carry on a non-verbal conversation with your horse that goes something like this: "I am asking you for a right-lead lope by my left heel pressure. No. No. No. Not a left-lead lope," you say as you pull the horse immediately back to a walk. "Left heel pressure means a right-lead lope. Good boy," you respond as the horse lopes off in a right lead as you release all pressure and sit quietly on his back.

> *Example:* If you correct a horse, whether or not the correction is intentional, you are telling him that he has done something wrong. If you accidentally bump his mouth when he departs into a lope, the next time you ask for a lope, he may refuse to lope at all because you "told" him that loping was wrong.

5. PERSEVERENCE
To train, you must have the perseverance and dedication to consistently and repeatedly explain to your horse what each cue means. By using the same cue in the same way for the same maneuver, over and over again, and by rewarding him for a proper response by sitting quietly and leaving him alone, he will learn in time what the acceptable response to each given cue.

> *Example:* Because you always ask a horse for a left-lead lope from your right-heel cue, he will understand that right-heel pressure only means a left-lead lope—it does not mean a right-lead lope.

6. THINK LIKE A HORSE
You need the ability to put yourself in a horse's place, or to "think like a horse." You must think of what you are telling a horse every time that you ride. The absence of a cue tells a horse that he is correct and that he should continue what he is doing. A correction tells the horse that he is wrong and therefore should change the behavior that caused him to get corrected. He must learn that you will consistently correct him over and over again until he gives in and performs as you have asked.

> *Example:* Your horse cuts into the center of the ring. To tell him that he is wrong, you must consistently pull him in two to three tight circles to the outside of the arena or in the direction he is trying to avoid as soon as he begins to cut into the center. He will soon understand that to avoid getting pulled into the tight circles he hates so much, he only has to stay on the rail and not cut in. However, if you do not correct him immediately, or if you let him get to the center of the arena before you correct him, he will not associate the correction with the "crime."

7. TRAIN STEP BY STEP
Never expect more of a horse than he can give at that particular point in his training. Just as a baby must first learn to crawl before he can walk, and walk before he can run, so must a horse first learn the basics before he can go on to the more demanding maneuvers.

> *Example:* You cannot expect a horse to slide to a stop before he learns how to elevate his shoulders, lock his hind legs underneath his belly, and paddle in a cadenced stop in front. Asking a horse to slide to a stop before he knows how will cause him to jam his front legs into the ground and bounce to a stop.

8. BE CONSISTENT

Consistency and the repetition of aids are very important. Show a horse what you want by using the same aids, in the same way, over and over again. By using the same cue in the same way to ask for the same response, a horse will understand exactly what is expected of him from that same cue.

> *Example:* To ask a horse to move just his hindquarters or his hip away from leg pressure, use leg pressure behind the girth. To ask a horse to move his entire body sideways, use your leg pressure at the girth. Don't expect a horse to read your mind and move his entire body sideways if you use your heel behind the girth, because you have already taught him that it means to move only his hip.

9. EXAGGERATE AT FIRST

When initially starting a colt, or teaching any horse a new aid, you generally have to exaggerate the aid at first and take it step by step.

> *Example:* When initially teaching a youngster to walk under saddle, squeeze both legs lightly to ask for a walk. If the colt does not respond to your asking aid, exaggerate your aid and make him uncomfortable by continuously bumping his sides with your heels until he does walk. As soon as he begins to walk, stop bumping and sit quietly. His reward for walking is that you sit quietly on his back and leave him alone when he walks. Because you initially ask for the walk by a light squeeze from your legs, and follow his inaction with the exaggerated bumping, the colt will soon respond to the light squeeze to avoid being bumped.

10. BUILD ON GROUNDWORK CUES

Use the cues you have previously taught your horse on the ground to help him understand new cues given on his back.

> *Example:* To teach a young horse to jog, squeeze both legs and cluck. Because the horse already knows that a cluck means to jog (from his longe-line training), it is easy for him to understand that a squeeze from both legs, combined with a cluck, means to jog. The only difference is that now the directions come from you on his back rather than from the center of the longeing circle. Using an "old" cue that a horse already knows and combining it with a new cue—the transition from obeying a cue on the ground to obeying a cue under saddle—is relatively easy for a horse to understand.

11. GIVE CUES CLEARLY AND CONCISELY

Your aids must be clear and concise to allow a horse to learn exactly what you want from each aid. Use your aids so that a horse can understand what you want, then reward him for acting correctly.

> *Example:* When teaching a horse to spin, you first elevate his shoulders to put his weight back over his hocks. Then, using your legs and neck-rein cue, and sometimes the direct-rein cue, you ask the horse to cross over in front and "spin." When a horse takes one crossover step, you release all pressure and reward him for that one step.

12. NEVER LET A HORSE LEARN THAT HE CAN IGNORE OR AVOID YOUR AIDS

Make it uncomfortable for your horse to be wrong or bad and comfortable for him to be right. Don't let a misbehavior go unchecked—it will become a bigger problem tomorrow.

> *Example:* You ask your horse to lope and he continues to walk. If you don't enforce the lope cue and *make* him lope, you have just taught him he can ignore your cues. He doesn't have to lope if he doesn't want to because he doesn't think you will make him. Once you ask for the lope, you are committed to getting it! You are the driver, not the passenger.

13. ASK AND THEN TELL

Although you generally have to exaggerate your aids when initially training a horse, you eventually want him to respond to light, barely seen aids—the end result of any training program. Ask and then tell a horse to teach him to respond to a light aid. First, ask him to respond using a light aid. Be sure to give him time to absorb and react to the asking aid (three seconds or so), but not so much time that he forgets your original request. If he does not respond to your "asking" aid, only then should you "tell" him to perform, using a stronger aid. Allow him to avoid the harsher "telling" aid by giving him time to respond to the "asking" aid. Be fair, consistent, clear and concise. Correct and reward immediately so that the horse can understand whether he is right or wrong. If he doesn't respond to the telling aid, *make* him respond.

> *Example:* Ask a horse to lope using light pressure from your outside heel (for an inside lead). If he does not lope, and you give him the time to absorb and then react to your request, bump him hard with your heel to tell him that he must lope now. If he still does not lope, use either a crop or spurs, as long as you have a secure lower leg that will not poke him unintentionally. In time, by repeating this sequence of "ask and then tell," the horse will respond to the light "asking" aid to avoid the harsher "telling" aid.

14. TRAIN EVERY TIME YOU RIDE

Finally, if you want to train a horse, you must commit yourself to riding like a trainer. A small problem left unfixed becomes a bigger problem the next time. You cannot allow a horse to act in an undesirable manner for five days, then kill him on the sixth for the same behavior. That confuses him and he will never learn what is acceptable. "Train" your horse every time you ride and be fair.

> *Example:* If you ask your horse to stop and stand and he walks forward three steps—and you don't correct him—expect him to try to walk forward four or five steps the next time you stop him. By letting him move forward without a correction the first time, you "told" him that he really didn't have to stop and stand. If he walks forward three steps, correct him by backing him six steps. Then ask him to stand again.

About the Author

Laurie C. Truskauskas Knott grew up in the town of Burlington, Connecticut, and began riding ponies at the age of three. As a young single parent, she went to work for Joe Ferro, one of the men responsible for setting up the Quarter Horse Association and a highly respected trainer of both reiners and jumping horses. And so began a long friendship that started Laurie on the road to training and writing about horses. From time to time, Ferro would mention that he wished he had written books so that all of the knowledge he had gained was not lost. One day, Laurie wrote an article and sent it to a national horse magazine where it ran as a feature spread. She has continued to write for numerous publications since, and published her first book, *Training the Two-Year-Old Colt*, in 2000.

About that time, Laurie took a trip to Texas to visit an old friend. Her dream had always been to move to a warmer climate and train horses. On the trip, she came across the farm of her dreams. Within a year she was resettled there, enjoying life, training horses professionally, giving lessons, writing books and articles, and basically living a dream.

Laurie's books and articles are frequently praised for presenting usable, easily understood step-by-step training methods. More books are in the works, and her greatest wish is that they help readers learn to be better horsepeople who think about what they are telling the horse in the equal, thinking partnership of horse and human.

Other Books by Laurie Truskauskas Knott:

Training the Two-Year-Old Colt
Covers halter breaking and handling a young horse on through the first saddling and the first trail ride.

Understanding Showmanship: Everything You Need to Know to Win in Showmanship Classes
Conditioning, outfitting and training the horse and handler for all types of showmanship classes.

The ABC's of Showmanship
A pocket-sized arena handbook with showmanship patterns you can practice.

Training for Trail Horse Classes: Train Your Horse to Compete Successfully
Makes training for this popular class easy with step-by-step instructions.

The ABC's of Trail
Pocket-size arena handbook containing practice patterns, checklists and tips.

The ABC's of Lope Overs
A take-to-the-practice-arena booklet with progressive exercises to help you and your horse master this most challenging trail maneuver.

Additional Alpine Titles You Might Enjoy:

Horse Anatomy, A Coloring Atlas. Robert Kainer, DVM, and Thomas McCracken, MS. An exceptional and unique way to learn horse anatomy, the physical systems of the horse, common ailments or conditions that may affect them, and why.

The Equine Arena Handbook: Developing a User-Friendly Facility. Robert Malmgren. If you want to set up a practice arena or revamp an old one that has poor drainage or footing, this book is a must!

Trail Training for Horse and Rider. Judith Daly. The complete book for recreational trail riders. Covers safety, trail hazards and obstacles, and how to condition, socialize and train a safe and dependable trail horse.

All of the above are available from:
Alpine Publications, P.O. Box 7027, Loveland, CO 80537
1-800-777-7257 • www.alpinepub.com • Fax 970-667-9157
Ask for them also at your favorite tack, feed or supply outlet or bookstore.